Don't Let Your Children Choose Your Nursing Home

A Guide for Planning Your Elderhood

Betty Halladay

Library of Congress Catalog Number:
ISBN 13: 978-0-6151432-3-1

Design and Layout by SelfPublishing.com

Printed in the United Sates of America

CONTENTS

ACKNOWLEDGMENTS

POSTHUMOUSLY, MY DEEPEST THANKS to my mother, aunt and mother-in-law for agreeing to experience the retirement resort life. It was total commitment on their parts and they lived it well.

Secondly, I am indebted to the Second 50 Years groups and the Last Resorts and Other Options class members, who showed up month after month with enthusiasm and support for the ideas we developed and the lifestyle we professed. You insisted that I publish this information, and for your encouragement I am very grateful.

To my editors, Dana Cole, Linda Ropes, Fran Stearns, Marcia Gladstone, Barbara Alderfer, and Jerry Halladay, you are wonderful. Thank you for your candid opinions and criticism. I did not always follow your advice, but I always appreciated it.

Again, to my ever patient husband, Jerry, who listened and listened and listened. I hope these ideas come to fruition for us together someday.

To Lois and Fritz Broman,
Betty Jane Pabst Alyn and Emily Halladay
with love and appreciation.
You would be so proud of my completion of this book.

PREFACE

WHY DID I WRITE this book? As I complete this first edition, it is 2007 and I am sixty-six. Members of my peer group are either trying to take care of their parents or are trying to decide how to plan their own future old age. The ones taking care of their parents are struggling to manage the lives of elders who have reached the point of needing physical help and mental supervision. The ones looking forward to their own futures are trying to decide what should be done, and when. Behind us all is a tidal wave of the baby-boomers who are approaching both of these conundrums.

Over fifteen years I guided four relatives (both of my parents, my mother-in-law, and my maternal aunt) through their elder years to their deaths. After my father's uncomfortable experience of dying at home, I encouraged the three remaining ladies, in turn, to move to a retirement community near my home. Through their eyes, I became an imbedded observer in retirement residences, hospitals, nursing homes, and small boarding homes. I listened to and talked with other residents, families and employees. I formed opinions about long term care insurance and guardianship of elders. I felt compelled to make notes and lists in order to remind myself of how to survive under these circumstances in my future.

I also discovered that most of my peers know very little about old-folks residences, and they have a horror of nursing homes. The new continuum-of-care residential communities seem frivolous and financially outrageous to them. They stretch their budgets to buy long term care insurance policies. They are unrealistic and procrastinating about the relative disability of old age.

To all of you I say – let's prepare ourselves. With knowledge about old age, and exploration of the eldercare marketplace, let's take control and not let our families have to solve these problems for us.

These are my experiences and current opinions, and this is an evolving topic. You should know that I have no relationship to any retirement organization other than the experiences I had through my elders. I expect you to consider my ideas, but to verify the specifics for yourself. This manuscript will be in a state of constant revision and update, and I would enjoy your input and comments.

> Betty Halladay
> 12637 W 6th Place
> Golden, CO 80401

INTRODUCTION

OLD AGE IS LIKE giving birth … or skiing a breathtaking slope … there is no other way out. At this point we have to stay the course.

In the retirement section at the bookstores are some new books that cause me concern. One is about adult children watching their parents for signs of Alzheimer's. Another is about these children choosing a nursing home for a failing, unappreciative relative. A third one is about adult children introducing discussion topics to help their elder decide to live in an assisted-living facility.

Don't Let Your Children Choose Your Nursing Home is about being a senior who takes the initiative before the children are forced to act. After all, who should be in charge?

We seniors know that most of us are living long, healthy, active retirement years. We travel, write, create, and volunteer. Our days are busy in ways our children know nothing about.

We also know that we forget where we put our keys or glasses. We don't remember why we went down to the basement. We are very careful to turn off the stove or iron. Sometimes we confuse appointments. Bladder control is becoming an oxymoron. We have to be very careful not to spill food on our clothes. We know we should hire someone to aerate the grass on the south side of the house and to prune the trees but we procrastinate endlessly.

We know our children are too busy to visit very often. The neighbors are beginning to keep an eye on us. And ... we know we are not going to get better. We know these things.

What are we doing about it?

Your neighbors, children, friends, and church committees should not have to concern themselves for your safety and well being. For short downtimes, yes. For the long term, no. After retiring from employment, after the traveling years and the volunteering, you reach a point late in life when you need help with everyday tasks: shopping, preparing meals, housekeeping, keeping clean, and washing clothes. At this point you are long past yard maintenance and house painting. Being this elderly might feel like recovering from the flu, you are always tired. You just cannot manage without help. And, if you put off setting up a safety-net of assistance for this future time, it will creep up on you. Family members and friends will be compelled to come to your aid, and your children may move you in with them.

What if you anticipate these needs before they are critical. You either need to have a plan for hiring regular assistance in your home; or you need to arrange for living accommodations where these services are provided. You could prepare while you have the energy to plan, evaluate, and effect the necessary changes.

It is a tragic mistake not to plan for our less productive older years. There are very attractive options. There are good solutions. All we need to do is know about them and take action. Long-term care insurance is not the solution. (See chapter 4, *Long-Term Care Insurance.*)

I cannot urge you strongly enough to take some very specific steps to plan for your elder years. You can make those years pleasing, comfortable, secure and satisfying. It is so easy to let the days go by only to find you have waited too long, and the options and decisions are out of your control.

The planning begins with these two starting points:

- What is your life expectancy as best you can predict? (See chapter 7, *When You Will Need What*)
- What are your resources/assets (including your long-term care insurance and it's specific coverage) and how could they best be utilized ? (See chapter 11, *Money from Where.*)

Here are four reasons that should motivate you to take action so as not to let your children take over your life:

- Your children really know little about your life. They don't know how you spend your days or what you would choose about many things.

- Though your children may know about retirement living or nursing homes, most do not. You have a vested interest in exploring these options.
- Your children don't have time to make these choices for you, or to take care of you long distance. They have busy lives of their own.
- There is the possibility of a conflict of interest that must be considered. It is their inheritance that you are spending lavishly or sparsely. It should be your choice, not theirs.

If I can persuade you to just take a look at the retirement residences in your area, I will have accomplished my intention. If you are determined to stay in your house, some planning information is also included. (Chapter 10, *You Are Staying Put.*)

Thanks for reading. Happy aging.

NOTES ON TERMINOLOGY:

I will refer to church and church members now and then. It has nothing to do with faith or religion. I believe that churches are our small towns — these are the people who know you and, perhaps, your family. They will come to your aid if necessary. When I refer to your church or to the church members, I mean your extended relationship with a larger group of people who know you and your needs — your support network.

I will refer to your children, and you may be childless. Please substitute a favorite relative or heir. If you are really family-free, this book's advice is all the more essential.

I am writing frequently as if you have a spouse. If it should be partner or roommate, or if you are single, again, these discussions and decisions may be even more urgent. Until our government extends the legal rights of spouses to all relationships, discussions and decisions about elderhood choices need to be defined, documented, and communicated without delay.

In the case of numbers throughout the book, they are supposed to be spelled out for correct usage, and I know that. However, where I have used them numerically, it is intentional for easier reference for the reader.

Part I

Planning
Your Elderhood

A.
YOU NEED TO DO THIS

1. IF YOU WERE OLD

OLD MAY FEEL LIKE a compliment before you are twenty-one, but it's an insult afterwards. Old can infer being worn out or a lack of usefulness. As no specific age is a milestone for old, let's specify some working terms to use for this book's conversation.

On these pages the term *senior* means you have enough years to get a discount: be that fifty, or fifty-five, or sixty or sixty-five. A senior is retired and active, one who may volunteer and travel. When I say senior, don't think age. There are folks who have reached eighty or ninety years who are just senior. As a senior, you need to establish control over the eventuality of being an elder through early planning. Otherwise, control is lost.

When I use *elder*, think of one who is senior, but who also has some need for assistance. Elders receive respect, and consideration, and an allowance for their frailty from the rest of us. They have mild disabilities that are age related. Being elder may be genealogical. In my family, you are elder at about eighty-five. In my husband's family, elder is at about age ninety. Some families have very short life spans where elder begins at about age seventy.

I use *aged* for those who need guidance and extensive help. The aged may be semi-aware of happenings around them. Senior and elder reflect ability and health issues but not age, whereas aged is likely to be reflective of mental capacity, largely impacted by age.

Plans for elderhood can be made at one of these three life stages:

1. Senior – when you are involved and can anticipate the changes.
2. Elder – when a change becomes necessary and is relatively forced upon you and your family.
3. Aged – when you have a major experience and someone else has to put the pieces together and do the planning.

Regardless of other details, this planning centers on where you will live. Supervision, assistance and health care, twenty-four hours a day if needed, are the major considerations.

If we were sitting together and talking about the problems of getting older, the following are some issues that we would discuss:

What is the problem? To start with, I'm sure you are getting tired of taking care of all of your "stuff." Agreed? You need to get rid of decades of accumulated belongings. How could you simplify your life and redirect your energy into other activities like social connections and creative pursuits? Fewer worries would be nice, less procrastination.

What could the problem look like? How about having difficulty with stairs and yard work, and not having as much energy as you used to have. Maybe your partner is not as able as he/she used to be. Perhaps the death of a spouse has made life very different, lonely. There may be a nagging distaste when you think of the prospect of living with your children. Things are changing, and definitely not for the better.

Whose problem is it? It is mostly yours now, but it will be your family's if you postpone taking action yourself. Your neighbors and friends may be showing signs of being more solicitous.

What are some solutions? One of your goals needs to be to see for yourself what community living looks and feels like as a senior/elder. What alternatives are out there? Would they be acceptable to you?

Why do you have to leave your house? You don't. You should investigate some alternatives. Communal living is not for everyone.

How do I know when I need help? It is hard to be objective about oneself and no one wants to be told they are mentally slipping. It might be a good idea to give a close, trusted friend permission to tell you if you are not coping well. This is difficult. Everyone forgets now and then and, after an injury, one needs time to heal. There is not a standard rule of knowing when long-term help is needed. It would be better to decide on a move before help is required, to move *to* something rather than *from* something.

What does a "cry for help" look like? It is obvious if it is extreme. A loss, injury or sickness may make a change necessary. A doctor could tell you it is time to get assistance. Could there be some earlier signs? Spoiling leftovers in the refrigerator, or a battered car, or confusion about time or appointments might be signs? Other signs may include loneliness, boredom, idleness, and depression.

Would you live with your children? Do they casually say, "Mom/Dad can live with us when the time comes." This my be the case, but when younger relatives take on the care of older relatives, the youngsters frequently sacrifice their own lives when trying to increase the quality of life for the elder. In the "agricultural" family, many generations were comfortable together. In the more modern two-professional-workers-with-children family, additional household members may or may not be beneficial. The nicest thing that you can do for your family may be to take on the responsibility of making a change while you are able to do it yourself, gracefully.

What residential solutions are available? This is the target of this book. Think location first. The area of your search should be focused on your current life, your family, your church. Where do you want to be? Whom do you want to be with and near? Is there someone you should be near for convenience?

What would you need to feel comfortable? What are your personal preferences about little things at this stage of life? What do you do with your day? You need to actually list what you know about yourself that will help you choose a satisfying solution. No one else knows.

How much money will it take? Comparisons need to be made concerning leaving a larger estate to your children versus spending more in taking care of yourself. You need simple worksheets for estimating available funds. (See chapter 11, *Money from Where*?) You could investigate both private pay facilities and those that are government subsidized.

Considering the proposal at this stage: your immediate goals should include determining what kinds of solutions are available and what they look like. Form a tour group of friends or fellow church members with common interests to do onsite visits of various assistance facilities. Your long term goals are to create a plan, and work your plan.

Compare opinions. Learn together. Be more prepared. Take action.

2. Consider
Resort Living

THERE IS A POPULAR story about an elderly lady on a cruise who was particularly catered to by the crew. Some of the other passengers asked about her and found that she had moved into a stateroom and lived there full time. She said it was cheaper than a nursing home and much nicer. Realistically, if she actually needed nursing home care, the cruise staff would not be able to provide that level of assistance. However, if she needed what is called independent living or assisted living, she could be quite comfortable on the ship, depending upon her needs. The ship provides entertainment, meals, housekeeping service, laundry service, moderate medical facilities, and general supervision.

Truthfully, getting older is frustrating. You need a hearing aid and you hope it does not show. You can't see without your glasses, which are in your pocket because

you don't need them all the time. You don't really want
to get up on a ladder to work on the house, but you make
yourself do it, carefully. Your kids volunteer to do the
driving, maybe because they don't trust yours. People get
impatient behind you in line if you are slower. You are
misunderstood when you try to explain something. You
volunteer, but you know you are not quite as competent
doing what you used to do easily. The doctor wants you
to use a cane or walker, in public! Everyone everywhere is
in such a hurry!

Worse yet, it's embarrassing to be a burden on your
family and friends. You feel apologetic if they have to use
their evenings and weekends tending to your needs. It is
so difficult to ask for a ride or accept food donations from
church members. If it is temporary, you can tolerate it and
reciprocate later, but not if it is long term.

Life is much less embarrassing or frustrating if you are
with your peers in a gracious environment where everything
is set up for your abilities. In a retirement community
you sign up for this "cruise" and don't look back. You are
welcomed at the gate. The folks on the "ship" are so kind,
they make allowances for you and assist your every need.
You can choose from a list of activities or you can relax and
watch the people walk by. The food is wonderful and the
"captain" welcoming. If you need assistance, it is not an
exception — everyone gets assistance. Your family knows
where you are and that you are in good hands.

This "cruise" is a few blocks away. Resort living is
available to you on dry land in your own neighborhood.
My use of the cruise or resort setting may seem repulsive to
those who see luxury as ostentatious, but in these vacation

settings, most of your needs are anticipated and met. At least give retirement living serious consideration. Make an appointment to tour and have lunch. Take a relative or friend. If you are pleasantly impressed, perhaps you can make arrangements to rent a guest apartment for a few days and make a trial run.

Make learning about and exploring retirement resorts a project worth your time. You need to know about these services in evaluating plans for your elderhood.

3. Protecting Your Estate

WHY WOULD YOU TAKE your hard earned and saved resources and spend them on a resort? Living upscale is not your style. Your home is paid for and, living there, you live well and within your means.

My mother said, "Money is stored-up labor. Spend it as if you had worked for it." No argument. I would also add: Your paid-for house is stored-up security. However, when you begin to depend on your neighbors, church, friends, and family for assistance, you are living on charity. Your stored equity is being hoarded while others labor to care for you for free. Some of them may inherit from you, but not most.

Well, your house is your children's inheritance. You do not want to spend it. You plan to buy services in order to stay in your house. That's okay. If your monthly income will cover purchased services, your house value is safe.

Imagine making this announcement to your heirs:

I'm going to live as conservatively as possible so that I can leave as much money for you as I can. I love you and I want to do this for you. I had to work hard for this and I want you to have more than I had. (Okay so far?) When I begin to need more help, now and then, and finally daily, I want you to take care of me. You can either come to my house, or I could move closer to you, or I could live with you. (No, you were going to stay home.) We could hire help. We will remodel my front porch so that a wheelchair can be rolled into the house. Some of my doorways will have to be made wider. My bathroom will need a walk-in shower. I might need a different table that is wheelchair friendly. If I become too difficult, you can just put me in a nursing home.

Now wait a minute!

At some point this starts to be ugly and expensive. Imagine this discussion with yourself:

Up until now, I have depended on my paid-for house to give me security. I have income which is meeting my present needs for cash. If I continue to stay here, however, at some point I will be dependent upon others for assistance. I could buy that assistance. But this house, which has been my sanctuary, could begin to be my prison if I can't get out without help. If I were to consider a retirement community, I would be taken care of as a routine matter. How could I best use my assets? I want to keep my estate relatively intact. I could consider a community where the value of my house is invested in a deposit that is wholly or partially refundable. I would be transferring my equity from house security to retirement security. If I did this, my income might just cover the monthly fee and cash expenses. These communities are becoming popular so this might be a safe investment. On the other hand, if I moved to a rent-based community, I could transfer my house security into an interest earning annuity and draw what extra I need monthly to meet my rent. Either one might be acceptable depending on other factors. Either way, my estate will shrink. Can I live with that? Would my heirs approve? They might be appreciative. It's worth consideration.

Now you are thinking. Gather some more information.

4. Long-Term Care Insurance

MANY YEARS AGO, DID you purchase a long-term care insurance policy? Or are you thinking of buying one? Every policy is unique. The words used, and what we thought they meant, may have changed through the years. Sit down with your policy and read it carefully. You will want to review the coverage with your insurance agent to be certain you understand exactly what the long-term care insurance terms used in the contract mean to that insurer. It is not news to you that the definition of terms can be used to deny coverage in any insurance policy.

As you read, take notes. What conditions are covered and for how long? What are the daily pay outs and the maximum pay out for your lifetime? Can the services be performed in a nursing facility or a nursing home or could the services come to your house?

If you have coverage for at-home help, you will want to be sure the retirement resort you are considering allows outside contractors to come into your space. Some residences provide services, like physical therapy, and will not allow other contractors to compete. If this is important to you, put "Outside contractors allowed" at the top of your residence evaluation worksheet (Chapter 17a, *Combination Checklist*).

I am uncertain of the value of these policies so I am openly skeptical. The purpose of these policies is to provide financial help if you are nursing-home frail, not just senior or elder and relatively well. Be sure you know exactly what your policy covers and how it will apply to your life and when. It is easy to overlook that it applies at the very end. If you stay in your house until the insurance becomes effective, is that what you want, and is that the best plan for your social and emotional well being between now and when you are eligible for coverage? This is my issue: Do you mean to be sacrificing experiences in your senior years in order to have long-term insurance coverage when you are frail?

You may know a little or a lot about long-term care insurance. This is a brief review of some of the basic issues:

Long-term care insurance becomes active when you are either delusional or having difficulty with personal life tasks like dressing, eating, and getting out of a chair. Nursing home care is usually covered but some policies also cover the same frailties if you are at-home or in an assisted-living residence. Long-term care insurance reimbursement is for the very end-of-life care when the services needed are expensive.

You buy long-term care insurance to protect your estate from exhaustion, especially if your estate has to cover expenses for two of you. If the first spouse's decline is covered by insurance, there is a remaining estate to support the surviving spouse. If both partners are covered, there is an estate remaining for the heirs.

You also expect long-term care insurance benefits to keep you out of Medicaid-supported nursing homes which may be less desirable than private-pay facilities. But, should your estate become exhausted, you need to keep in mind that Medicaid will probably be there to pick up the cost of nursing care should you need it. There will be a bed for you somewhere. You will probably be too delusional to know a lot about where you are. Unpleasant thought now, but probable and important.

There are some other societal forces that affect long-term care insurance:

We all know that Medicaid is not prepared for when the baby-boomers reach nursing home age. Because of this reality, our government wants you to buy long-term care insurance. Companies have been encouraged to promote the long-term care insurance business. Thus, you have been encouraged to buy long-term care insurance and you may own a policy.

Because making a profit for shareholders is their reason for being, insurance companies write policies that favor their interest. Unless more is collected from the policy holders than is paid out, there will be no company left to honor the obligations – basic business practice.

There are several ways for the companies to prosper:

- Narrow the eligibility factors to avoid paying out benefits. If your conditions do not qualify, you are not covered. Since few of us are experienced in predicting the needs of elders, nor do we fully understand technical contracts, it is difficult for you to know if your policy will be appropriate when you need it.
- Increase the premiums through the years. If you can no longer afford your policy, it lapses.
- Negligent billing for benefits. When you are eligible for coverage, it is probable that you will not be a competent administrator of your own paperwork. Lacking a competent care manager, you may receive neither adequate care nor full compensation, especially if you are living in your own house. If you reside in an assisted-living facility or nursing home that accepts insurance payments, you will receive assistance from staff who are experienced in taking care of residents and in processing claims.

And, if your insurer does not prosper, it goes out of business, perhaps transferring your policy to another company.

There are good reasons to have long-term care insurance. My argument, however, is that if you can afford the policy, you could probably do without it. Granted your heirs might inherit less. But my biggest objection is that if you are in a position to barely afford the policy, you may lose the whole thing if you skip a payment. Meanwhile, you will most certainly miss out on other life-enriching experiences that you might have enjoyed if you had had the money available.

Why save money to house yourself in a nicer nursing home when all you will need at that time is a warm place to sleep and food to eat? I hope for many letters on this subject. This is not professional advice. I am not a consultant. You may find me in a Medicaid nursing home some day under delusions of revising this book. Nonetheless, this is my opinion at this writing.

5. PARTICULARLY FOR MEN

IS IT AN UNDERSTATEMENT that retirement-home talk is distasteful for most men? Your home is your castle, your sanctuary, your cave. It establishes your territory as a male beast on this planet. It represents your accomplishments in the material world. Even thinking about cashing out on this asset while you are an able-bodied male senior alarms and depresses you.

Guys, I'm going to try to change your mind just a little. Is it possible that you could maintain territory in a different way? It is important to you to take responsibility for your own and your spouse's well being. No argument. You should continue to fulfill your role as leader of the family. At the same time, home maintenance really does get physically more difficult. Could you make a mental transition from (a) using your skills and your tools to get tasks done to (b) hiring that work done while you act as overseer? You become the boss rather than the worker.

At first, this means not risking your life cleaning out gutters, trimming trees, or painting eaves from a ladder. It means knowing from whom you can get what, done quickly and well. For example, our eighty-four-year-old neighbor hires a professional lawn service. A team of three men in a truck parks at the curb, unloads equipment, mows, trims, blows the sidewalk clean, reloads and drives away in six minutes flat. We neighbors are impressed with their speed and we admire the neighbor for taking care of this responsibility.

If this seems acceptable, then you might begin thinking about retirement community living in a different way. As a homeowner, you have always shared services from the water company, the telephone company, and the trash collectors. You either contracted to have this work done or paid your share while the community provided the service. What if you expand this idea to a community where there is food service, housekeeping, laundry, and health care support provided? The staff works for you and you receive the service. You pay your share. You take part in the resident council as well as the social activities. You become a contributing member of a different community.

Another eye opener: If you, the king of the castle, become less able, your lady becomes your caregiver. She may be a wonderful caregiver, or she may not be. Further, the lady of the house should not have to care for you by herself. There is lifting, steadying, feeding, bathroom visits, bathing, and night medications. Your last years, as well as hers, might be safer and more comfortable in a safety-net community where extra help is automatically provided when it becomes necessary. As the head-of-household, unpleasant as it seems, a man needs to take responsibility for planning his own demise.

My father was the nurse for our family, so when it became my mother's job to care for him twenty-four hours a day, he was in a precarious position. She did not have systematic, rational, middle-of-the-night caregiving skills. I was partly responsible for my dad's predicament. He always sought out my advice and I didn't know then what I know now. When he was diagnosed with prostate cancer, I supported his choosing alternative remedies, so he took zinc supplements for a long time before his cancer metastasized. He refused chemotherapy and elected to die at home. It was a difficult death, very painful, with mother trying to be his caregiver. Fortunately, there was a hospice nurse helping out at the end.

If I had it to do over, I would give my parents very different advice. I would have urged them to move to a retirement community where his health would have been monitored. He would have had more professional information and peer support to make his decisions. He might have agreed to surgery and had more years to enjoy. He might have died in a familiar nursing wing where he was known and loved. It was too easy for him to let Mom have her way about staying in their apartment condominium rather than carefully considering the advantages of reestablishing their home in a supportive, safety-net environment.

I also learned that well-intentioned, emotional family members may not be the ultimate in deathbed companions. If you have a cancer or some other debilitating condition, you need professionally skilled people to ease your discomfort. If you are in a hospice environment with assistance at every turn of events, death may come much easier.

And what if you become a widower? What if, rather than living at home alone and lonely, or finding another wife, you move to a retirement community. I'm serious. Think about it. Your meals are down the hall in the dining room. Someone cleans your apartment and changes your sheets. You can make arrangements for laundry. There is scheduled entertainment and you are surrounded by men and women who are your peers. You don't have to drive at night, or any time. Your children stop worrying about you. Wouldn't you rather be playing pool with a couple of guys, or watching a game with some cheering fans, than being home alone and the object of the neighborhood's concern? You need to see for yourself.

I challenge you men to explore elder communities. You could invite a buddy, and together, do some investigating. It's like buying a car. All you have to do is walk onto the lot (actually, into the reception area, like in a hotel) and someone will come to you and give you a sales pitch. Tell them I sent you. Show them this book. Tell them you are just shopping. If they ask you to stay for lunch, and the place feels fairly comfortable, do it. Don't buy the first one you look at. Give them your card and get a brochure with the manager's name. You will be on their mailing list by morning. When you receive invitations to various activities, go and check out your first impressions.

When you do move in, I have a special assignment for you. Make it your objective to brighten each day for every woman you meet. Smile, hold doors open, say hello and call her by name if you know it. If you do this, your days will be nicer, and so will those of the people around you. Don't be surprised if you get a few proposals of marriage, but keep this speech in mind, "Thank-you Doris, I am really flattered. You are such a sweetheart to ask, but I'm not going to marry again. Thank-you so much for thinking of me. If I change my mind I'll let you know."

Being a single man in a community of mostly women isn't bad. If you should decide to remarry, you must be able to talk about money. Prenuptial agreements are a must. Couples at this age frequently do not marry because one or the other would lose benefits from a previous marriage. Interestingly, the adult children may or may not object. It is a complicated subject worthy of much discussion with your intended.

If you do not intend to live with your children, do not wait for them to force a residence decision on you. It is not their decision. It is yours. Your life will end more delightfully and peacefully if you make a plan and work your plan.

6. RETIREMENT INDUSTRY VOCABULARY

THE FOLLOWING WORDS ARE tossed around as if everyone knows what is meant. New ones will be introduced around the country, but let's use these for basics. They have some defined constants but expect differences.

Patio homes are individual houses or single-story attached units where the landscaping and exteriors are maintained by the association. They are, in fact, condominium complexes or gated communities which are restricted to senior citizens. There may be social activities arranged by the association.

Independent living usually means cottages, attached or free standing, or full apartments. There is vehicle parking and a community room(s). Meals are not usually part of the package but may be available for a fee. There may be some housekeeping provided or offered for a fee. Sometimes you can have assistance services delivered to your unit. The residence may require that you use their contract staff for services such as physical therapy or a visiting nurse. No state license is required.

Assisted living is usually in apartments or suites. Meals, housekeeping, assistance with bathing and dressing are all provided, sometimes with an additional fee for each service. A registered nurse may be present only during the day. There may be caregivers on duty twenty-four hours. A state license is required.

Personal Care Boarding Homes are assisted living services but the term is used frequently to refer to homes on a much smaller scale. These small group homes may vary from two residents to ten or more. Services include room and meals, laundry, bathing and dressing, grooming, medication and twenty-four hour supervision. Nurse visits may be scheduled but no nurse is on duty. A state license is required.

Skilled Nursing, abbreviated in manuals as SKN, in a nursing home is really hospital care in a non-hospital setting. A registered nurse is on duty twenty-four hours and a medical doctor makes rounds during the week. Meals, housekeeping, laundry, bathing, and dressing are all included. Beds are usually of the hospital type with power back and knee lifts. Rooms are almost always shared. Providing nursing care is a far more expensive operation and is extensively regulated by the state. A state license is required.

Alzheimer's units are secure, that is they have locked doors to the outside because residents tend to wander. There is a secured outside yard. Residents have individual bedrooms and a common living area. Meals, housekeeping, bathing, and dressing are provided. Care is tailored to the individual needs of each resident. A state license is required.

Continuum-of-care residential communities (CCRCs) are complexes that have independent, assisted, nursing and Alzheimer's units all on the same campus. By popular demand, these are the residential resorts of the modern day. Older communities are remodeling to include all four services. The advantage for the resident is not having to make a move if your level of ability changes, called aging in place. This term is not completely accurate because in most of these residences, the population and the assistance is segregated by abilities. If you become incapacitated and are reevaluated from independent to assisted, you will probably move to a new apartment or room. You will also move to nursing when that is necessary. You do move, but on the same campus which you will be familiar with and thus it is not as confusing. Your friends will be making the same transitions and your more able neighbors and spouse can keep track of your move easily. There are a very few residences which are true aging in place where the services come to you and you do not move. Be aware, where this is offered, that this is a tricky balancing act on the part of staff. There are also some CCRCs that do not have skilled nursing facilities; they are using the name but not in its technically correct sense. Providing skilled nursing is very expensive and they are cutting that cost.

There are inconsistencies from these definitions. One independent-living facility allows wheelchairs, while another classifies them as assisted living. One independent living has a meal program; another has no dining room and residents must shop and cook for themselves. All assisted living services have meal programs, with some included in the rent, and some pay as you use. Some assisted services have twenty-four hour caregivers, while others only have someone who can be called on a beeper. Generally, independent living has additional services available, while assisted living can be remarkably independent. It depends on the management and the available staff.

Independent, assisted, nursing and Alzheimer's services are available in various combinations with emphasis on one, maybe two. Wherever the emphasis is, that is where the activities are focused. Be conscious of the emphasis. If you are mentally agile and choose a residence where the emphasis is on assisted, you may not receive the activity level you expect but, if you need lots of assistance, this may be an appropriate place.

When you visit a residence it will be apparent what the emphasis is by the population. If the marketing director shows you 24 independent units, 88 assisted units, and 30 Alzheimer beds, it is obvious that the emphasis is on assisted living. In this example, the activities for assisted residents may be more varied, due to the independent influence, but within the abilities of the assisted. If the population were reversed, 88 independent and 24 assisted, the activities may be geared toward the more active elder and beyond the abilities of some assisted residents. When you have visited a few residences and looked at their activities schedule, this will become more meaningful.

Retirement facilities may vary in payment options. Most facilities collect rent on a monthly basis. Most contracts may be broken with a 30-day notice.

A buy-in facility is another option. In the future we will see a vast number of CCRCs built in the Midwest as they are already very popular on both coasts. Additionally, complexes are being developed which are independent senior-living apartments offering deluxe floor plans and multiple common rooms. They include association employees who coordinate activities and operate the facility. These communities require a deposit which can be called many different things, but what is meant is that you buy your unit and then pay fees for communal services, very much like condominium association fees. You will be offered various returns on your money, 50%, 80%, 90%, some with interest, that becomes part of your estate upon your death.

Frequently you can buy in at two different levels. The higher level reduces your monthly fee more than the lower level. The high option is to assist those who are income poor and asset heavy. However, the two parts of the purchase may not be equal in interest earned. Read the contract carefully. It may be in your best interest to buy at the lower level and invest the rest of your capital where you control the interest and can make monthly draws.

Consider this arrangement a condominium purchase. Realize that there is probably no reserve of money to reimburse you if you decide to move out. Your unit must have a new resident whose deposit/purchase price reimburses you. If the complex has lost desirability for some reason, a new resident will be less easily found.

CCRCs are a new concept for inheriting children. When a senior buys into a complex that has a complete continuum, the children find themselves left with two choices when the end nears:

(a) leave mom/dad where they are, and the contract intact, and fly in to visit through the end, or

(b) move mom/dad closer, try to break the contract, and cash out the investment.

In a consultant capacity, I was contacted by the children of a couple who had bought into a CCRC in Arizona. Both the children and I reside in Colorado. Dad was not doing well and the children felt they should take on some responsibility, but they had no understanding of the CCRC. Mom was having trouble communicating the financial arrangement that she and dad had signed, and the daughter was referred to me for advice. I reviewed the CCRC idea with the daughter, and she was then informed enough to go to Arizona and decide which action would be best for the family.

If you buy into a CCRC, choose the location with your family in mind. Read the fine print to discover what your options are should you want to break the contract or should you want to stay on to the end despite your children's wishes. Some of these contracts are very attractive, granting elders complete care to the end of life even if their funds are exhausted. Of course, in this case, the amount left available for the estate will be minimal, if any. You might be quite content to live day to day in your choice of residence, letting the children make arrangements to visit as they may. It's your life, and your money.

What if you would not be interested in investing your principle in a complex at this time in your life? You feel your money would be much safer in a personal investment of your own with monthly draws that enable you to pay your rent in a pay-per-month community where you can give a 30-day notice and move out. No problem. There may be CCRCs in the community which are rent supported. If this is your point of view, these are more desirable and less risk to your financial and mental state if you should decide to make a change.

7. When You Will Need What

In this chapter I am trying to describe a comparable experience that will help you visualize what kind of safety net might be necessary in your future and, most importantly, when.

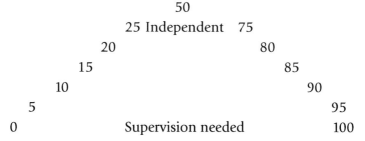

```
                        50
                  25 Independent   75
              20                        80
           15                              85
         10                                  90
       5                                        95
     0                 Supervision needed        100
```

Let this diagram be the human life span rising and then falling with the degree of independence exercised in various age brackets during a lifetime of 100 years. It may seem self-explanatory but the details are useful.

It is difficult to imagine yourself as less capable and less responsible than you are today. It is human nature to view yourself as always becoming more competent, not less. Losing ground is disorienting.

In a very general way your early years can be compared with your final years. For instance, at 75, your maturity and decision making abilities might be compared with those you had at age 25. You were an adult. You had a good comprehension of your responsibilities. You were a good driver; made reasonable plans for your daily life, planned vacations, and took care of your possessions. You took part in your community. You were firmly anchored, and so you are at 75.

Remember being 20? Perhaps you were a bit headstrong. Maybe you made impulsive decisions that worked out relatively well. You may have spent money a bit recklessly. Perhaps relatives kept their opinions to themselves as you told of career and marriage plans that seemed a bit outlandish from their point of view. How similar was this to your parents or other relatives at age 80? They were traveling or volunteering or investing in something. You hoped someone was keeping an eye on them or at least advising them. Probably they couldn't get into too much trouble. You encouraged them. After all, they had 80 years of experience to rely on.

Could your early teens compare with age 85 as a time of being a little headstrong without hurting your ego too much? You had a big ego at 15; drove a little carelessly at 16. You resented explaining your decisions to your parents. You usually looked presentable and took care of your own grooming. You were relatively on time for events. Did your parents try to monitor your plans and who you would be with? There was definitely a struggle of wills going on. Have you ever tried to persuade an 86 year-old uncle or father to do what you wanted him to do without provoking opposition?

How about age 10 and age 90? Someone had to provide your 10 year-old self with transportation. You chose your own clothing and dressed yourself, sometimes not too appropriately. You could bathe safely, after being told to do it, and you had to be reminded to clean up the bathroom. If you prepared food in the kitchen, usually a parent monitored your progress. You were sometimes more childlike and sometimes more like an adult. Could this be a similar picture, perhaps a bit more confused, at age 90? I remember dressing or re-dressing my 89 year-old mother before taking her somewhere.

Someone always monitors 5 year-olds. They may get their clothes on backward or inside out; they need their food cut up for them, and they need a bib; and they might scald themselves in the bath so are not allowed to bathe unsupervised. Perhaps at age 95, you will not go out alone, will need your food cut up, and could scald yourself in the shower.

We don't leave 2 year-olds unsupervised. They need to be fed, bathed, dressed. They may put anything down the toilet. They may leave the house in inappropriate clothing, maybe none. We love them, but we watch them, always. At 98, you hope there will be someone lovingly watching over you.

This model applies, in a very general way, to the diminishing of mental competence as you age. For the most part, at age 75, you are in a strong decision-making frame of mind. At age 85, you have less decision-making power and may need the support of a younger person. At age 90, you need daily, maybe constant, supervision.

How long will you live? Realistically, most of us don't live to be centenarians. By choosing the relative you most nearly resemble, you can estimate your genealogical end-of-life age. You can anticipate Alzheimer's or not. You can forecast likely age-related diseases or continued health based upon your family tree. By putting this estimated age idea together with the decline in responsibility idea, you can estimate both your end-of-life supervision needs and your terminal age. You can formulate a reasonable guess.

Ponder this: if your health history suggests a shorter life span, your responsibility factor probably continues to coincide with a life of 100 years. For instance, an elder who dies of heart failure at 89 does not necessarily exhibit more childish behavior than his/her longer lived peer at the same age.

If you would consider resort living, how about moving to a safety-net elder residence between ages 75 and 80? You would have the mental faculties to enjoy the change, the health to take part, the interest in learning a new lifestyle, the energy to make friends, and the faith of your children that you can make a good decision. If you wait until age 85, the children or guardians are already keeping an eye on your decision and this is good, but you will have lost 10 years of being independent in that resort setting. Those 10 years could have been some of the most relaxed and worry-free years of your life.

For couples, what if there is an age difference between you? If one of you is senior to the other by a decade, this difference in age may become as contrasting as it would have been in childhood. What does a 75 year-old spouse have in common with an 85 year-old? Well, love and a long-life experience together. When you were 65 and 75 it was as comfortable as 25 and 35. However, 75 and 85 compare with 15 and 25, calling for some extra effort by both partners. Factor in some health issues, and you have a complicated life-planning exercise.

It seems unreasonable to decide to move to a safety-net housing situation when it is so clearly unneeded today, at least for one of you. However, these prediction ideas may motivate you to start planning the next phase of your life together. If your age difference is by 10 years, perhaps a move when you are 75 and 85 would make sense. The younger of you would be flexible enough to handle the multitude of changes while at the same time easing the discomfort for the elder. Believe me when I say 85-year-olds do not want change in their lives. Your best bargaining issue may be for the elder to agree to moving as a benefit to the younger partner in order to save him/her from making the change alone when the elder is gone.

If you have 15 years or more difference, discuss the prospect of the younger needing some support when the elder begins to take more naps and becomes easily confused. Imagine the situation when the younger begins to take on serious caregiving responsibilities while you are living at your house. Help is through a relative, neighbor or emergency services. It would be very uncomfortable for the elder to need professional help and have to travel many miles away. In a retirement community, assistance would be available by a call button, even at night. It might be important to choose a facility with continuum of care to accommodate vastly different needs in service for each of you.

Talk this over, again and again. Imagine some specific scenarios that could happen and the possible outcomes. If you factor in the minimum age of 70 for residence in some communities, you may find options are limited. You have a strategic decision to make.

7A. Age Prediction Worksheet

This chart is the completion of this sentence: Person 1 most clearly resembles what relative, who died of what, at the age of what. Other life-shortening factors that either you or your relative might have experienced could include: cancers, heart disease or other chronic illness that could be noted.

Also, complete the prediction for person 2.

It is only a guess, but it could be useful as you determine an approximation of how many years your estate needs to be extended.

	Person 1 (you)	Person 2 (your spouse)
Most closely resembles what relative:		
who died of:		
at age:		
Other factors:		
Cancer		
Heart		
Chronic illnesses		

8. It's Time to Move

WHEN YOU PUT OFF planning and the years are passing by, what clues might signal when you need to get serious about a change?

1. Does this sound like you?

- You like to walk to some close destinations like a park, the library, or the grocery store.
- You drive your car well, and need the freedom to go and do activities.
- You are a member of several groups that meet regularly.
- You enjoy being involved at church.
- Your house reflects your life and tastes.
- You get outdoors often.
- You are doing something creative: art, music, or crafts.

- You enjoy cooking and sharing your results with others.
- You are in touch with your family and grandchildren.
- You are using your hearing aids.
- Your vision prescription is up to date.
- You have a system for taking your medications that works.

However, you have senior moments such as:

- You are forgetful, maybe more that you used to be.
- You have moments of being confused, and are embarrassed when you realize it.
- You are staying organized, generally.
- You have moments when driving when you have to concentrate to know where you are.
- You are beginning to find life to be more complicated.
- You are having small difficulties driving, such as nudging curbs, walls, or trash containers.

2. How much of this sounds like you?
- You no longer enjoy keeping house. Cleaning showers, tubs, and toilets is difficult. Dusting, vacuuming, and clean sheets are just too much bother.
- You are procrastinating. Maintenance on the house exterior and yard is getting out of control. Weeds are taking over.

- You find no one to talk with. The neighbors are busy, no guests come by.
- You are just bored. You would do more things, but you just don't get around to it and life goes by.
- You are telling your family you are happy this way, but the days are really long.
- You fall asleep watching TV or at your computer. Your day gets away from you.
- You think about being creative but nothing is really happening.
- You are taking your prescriptions ... most of the time.
- You get confused but can usually figure things out.
- You enjoy a good conversation, talking with strangers is no problem.
- You are reading more than you used to, maybe falling asleep over a book.

Any of this true about you?

- You rarely eat breakfast, just drinking coffee, maybe juice. Eating alone is not enjoyable.
- You are not outdoors much. Well, what is there to do and you might fall.
- You need curb service and a ride. Walking very far is exhausting.
- You refuse invitations to go out. You are afraid you might be knocked down in a crowd.

- You are alone, maybe lonely. The quiet is deafening.
- You wear the same outfit for days because it is just easier. It's not really dirty.
- You need a haircut but have not made an appointment.
- You are paying your bills but it seems like there is frequently a late charge, a mix-up.
- You are enjoying wine or scotch more than you used to, even early in the day.
- You are okay, but you are concerned about your spouse.

The first list is about independent living. You could stay in your house for a few more years or you could move to a retirement resort now and really enjoy it's opportunities.

The second list describes an increasing need for something to happen. Your life is not fun and you are not doing something about it. You could take the initiative or just wait ... until the family or neighbors realize something is wrong and take over. Not a good choice.

You need to do something, now!

If you decide to stay in your house, there are options:

- You could join the local senior center and go there every day. They might pick you up, and it would give you something to do.
- You could hire part-time help. Someone coming in would give you a bit of conversation as well as attention. You would need a relative to be the employer to handle the payroll and supervision

of what you expect the person to do. Chapter 10, *You Are Staying Put,* has a list of services that may need to be purchased.

If you would consider a last resort, do it:

- Move to a retirement community and get involved in a new life — friends, meals, activities, and a safety net. It really is a last resort and you need to do it, now.
- Do you need a low income resort? There are both subsidized independent apartments and subsidzed assisted living residences. You may have been driving past one for years and never known what it was. Get a friend to help you shop. Drop in and apply. Talk to the manager at one of them. Chat with a resident. Get on waiting lists, more than one. It may take a couple of years to get in, but it's worth it.

Do you need help? If you have waited too long and are not in a decision making mode, it will be difficult to make a good choice. Get someone trustworthy who knows you well to help in this decision.

A Timely Truth

You need to know this. If it is your intent to move to independent living but you want to wait until it is absolutely necessary, you are at odds with yourself — you cannot have it both ways.

Independent living means that: independent. You can walk, you can think, you can adjust to a new environment.

When you are considered as a prospective resident you must pass a physical. Your personal doctor must sign off that you are mentally and physically competent for independent living. Additionally, the facility's resident nurse or staff counselor will evaluate your current state of being.

I was shocked to learn of this process when my mother-in-law needed retirement living. She had to be seen by a geriatric physician and interviewed by the facility nurse before they would accept her as a resident. I was desperate to find her a shelter and they wanted me to take her to a doctor first! Arranging these appointments took days while she slept on our living-room couch. They finally accepted her, but not into independent living, even though she had been living by herself successfully recently. While a nursing home would have accepted her unconditionally, I did not think she needed skilled nursing care.

The residence has to do this. If they just rented an apartment without any evaluation of the occupant, they would take on individuals with emotional and physical duress that they are not prepared to handle. You do not want neighbors who are a danger to themselves or others. The residence is responsible for all that goes on under its roof.

If you wait until you are sure you need assistance, be sure you are thinking assisted living, not independent living. In assisted, you will be surrounded with other folks who need assistance. The social activities and mental stimulation will be at a reduced level. If, however, you move sooner into independent, you are accepted there and not overly evaluated as you slowly age. The mental stimulation of independent keeps you independent. The surroundings of assisted support your being assisted.

Be advised. This is why you research last resorts. Don't get caught waiting too long.

9. Moving is Overwhelming

HOW DO YOU GET it done? How do you move all of your stuff out of your house and into a new place? How do you get rid of the things you don't want. It's just not worth the hassle. It looks hopeless and you clearly can't do it.

What if you were on a tour and the director told you there was a very special event happening the last week of the tour ... but you would have to pack a small bag with just enough clothing for that last week. You could leave the rest of your belongings where they are. Would you pack a little duffle and go?

When you move to the resort you get to enjoy that special event: good food, entertainment, social activities and conversation. You spend your days doing what is important to you. Life is a piece of cake.

Guess what? You do not have to pack and unpack. There are people whose business it is to help you pack and unpack in your new place. They will make your bed, refill your medicine cabinet, and even transfer staples to your new refrigerator.

You do not have to move any of your stuff. There are professional movers just waiting to be told what few items you want moved. You can postpone closing your house for weeks or months until you decide you have what you need.

You do not have to have a garage sale. It takes energy and hours to sell household belongings at your curb. There are companies whose business it is to sell the rest of your stuff (after your family takes what they want) and get as much money as possible for it, and then send you a check.

You do not have to work to sell your house. That same company that sold all your stuff will clean, paint and sell your house. They want to get a good price and thus they will work for it.

When you were younger you did everything yourself. You rented a truck, moved heavy furniture, packed and unpacked boxes, and scrubbed and polished. You don't do that in your senior years, you hire it done. When you tour residences in your community, ask for references for moving companies that perform these services locally. A good marketing director will offer these referrals without your having to ask.

In chapter 18, *What Goes With You*, I'll give you some ideas on downsizing. It's no joke. It's a huge job. Best get started.

Find that senior resort that pleases you and move.

10. You Are Staying Put

YOU SIMPLY ARE NOT going to retirement residence living, and that is final. Be sure to make plans with your future guardian for supervision as you age. Plan it together knowing that it can be an awkward time. Be prepared. Do not get caught in the lurch by unexpected events.

Staying in your house can work. Here is a successful example. My friend Janet's mother, Mabel, lived to be 101. Mabel was healthy and took no prescriptions. Janet paid three ladies who cared for Mabel in her own home for over twelve years. They were there at different times of the day, gently offering food, helping her dress, and carefully bathing her and putting her to bed. Nothing was forced on her. Janet paid their salaries and arranged social gatherings for birthdays and holidays. This plan evolved from when Mabel's husband was alive and she needed help in caring for him. After several tries, a very acceptable caregiver was found. Mabel was a good employer/manager.

After her husband's death this caregiver continued on caring for Mabel as she aged. Two other caregivers were located, forming the triage of care. This was a successful plan, although Mabel spent little time with anyone but her caregivers and her daughter for many years. She slowly slipped to fifty-nine pounds and quietly passed away. These competent caregivers became more like family as the years went by. It was a good plan with responsible participants, an ideal situation.

Here is an example that did not turn out so well. Margaret had difficult adult children and a sizable estate. For financial security she put a living trust on her main house and sold her other properties. Because she had regular help in her house, she was not alone during the week and she managed alone on weekends. She was still driving. She planned to live there until death. However, as her health began to fail, she was not so comfortable being alone on weekends. Her granddaughter, Terri, needed a place to live while she was attending college, so she moved in. Terri fixed meals for Margaret on weekends and kept an eye on her in the evenings. Then Terri developed a serious outside relationship. She loved her grandmother, but her attention was divided. She would get a quick meal for Margaret, help her to bed, and then leave for most of the night or for a couple of nights. Margaret no longer had the safety net she needed. Coincidentally, Margaret's sister was moving to an independent living resort which also had assisted living services. Margaret let her house go to the trust and moved to assisted living. Luckily she had the means and the mental faculties to develop a second plan.

Perhaps the lesson is to do the best long range planning possible, but realize that nothing is foolproof. Try to have a second plan in mind if the original support plan fails.

If you are going to arrange for care in your house over time, you can slowly begin to provide for these services:

- Yard maintenance. Someone needs to hire yard work done, or do it themselves. The house, as well as the lawn and plantings, need maintenance.
- Housekeeping. Someone needs to scrub bathrooms, dust, vacuum, clear furniture surfaces of clutter, and take out the trash. Perhaps this person should also change the linens.
- Food and groceries. Someone needs to shop, take charge of the refrigerator contents, and prepare meals and snacks.
- Laundry. Someone needs to wash, dry, fold, and put away clothes, bed linens, and towels, and manage any dry cleaning needs.
- Appointments and transportation. Someone needs to help make appointments and drive the elder to professional offices. Eventually someone needs to have a health services power of attorney.
- Personal Hygiene. Someone needs to help with weekly bathing at a minimum. The elder will need monitoring for personal hygiene and grooming, including haircuts.
- Social needs. Someone needs to see that friends come to call and that the elder has the option to get to church or other meaningful gatherings.

All of these services will not be needed immediately, unless there is a personal crisis. However, gradually all of these services need to be provided.

B. Means to
Justify the End

11. Money From Where?

JUST EXACTLY HOW MUCH money do you have available for resort living? You may have more (or less) than you think, but you need realistic numbers for planning.

This chapter will guide you through a simplistic method of analyzing your income and assets. Approximate figures will serve this purpose. There is nothing hard to compute in this format, and it is complete enough to give you an estimate of your elderhood finances. At the end of the chapter is a suggested worksheet.

1. List your monthly income(s).

If you are a couple, use the 2 people column for the time you are both living. Use the 1st person and 2nd person columns for the surviving partner in each case.

Use monthly figures. Social Security and pensions are already monthly. Check your pension retirement contracts. What does each survivor receive? If one is gone, does the survivor still get all of the other's pension or just part of it? These figures may be different because of decisions you made at the time of retirement.

Compute the three totals for each column: 2 people, 1st person, and 2nd person. If you are single now, you only need one column. These are monthly income figures and do not include any of your invested reserves.

2. Enter your assets: your investments, any reserves and the value of your house(s).

The investments and house assets do not need to be exact. Make them conservative and realistic. There may be some assets that belong to one or the other of you if you are a couple. Put everything in its appropriate column.

Next, compute the total value of assets.

3. From your total value of assets figure(s), determine how much of your assets could be drawn per month for the remainder of your years. Assume each person lives to age 100 for now.

Example: Let's say you have total assets (sale of house and stock market investments) of $300,000 and you are age 80, and plan to live to age 100. If you die sooner, the remainder, and the accumulated interest, goes to your children. If you live 20 years (age 80 to 100) you could spend $15,000 per year ($300,000 divided by 20). Divide that by 12 months per year and you could draw $1250 per month from your assets.

Now you have two useful totals: your monthly income, and a monthly draw from your assets.

4. Add your monthly income to your monthly draw and you have your estimated monthly allowance for resort living.

There are some truths to be acknowledged here: you probably won't live to 100; nursing care will cost lots more than resort independent living; and we are making plans to spend the principle, carefully. If we use calculations that plan for you to stay until age 100 and you leave at 90, the last couple of years may be nursing home years and more expensive but your budget for the last 10 years (age 90 to 100) will easily cover the increase. So, nursing home is covered. Your children still get whatever principle is left, including any interest. If you have long-term care insurance, these last years are where it is most likely to apply.

So far, this example is purposefully simple. Our quick method leaves the interest and unexpended balance to the children. I do not mean to be glib about the interest earned on investments, as it can be a sizable amount, but complicated computations cause some people to give up the whole exercise or procrastinate, and you don't have time for that.

To calculate a more exact amount, including interest and inflation, go to this Web site:

http://www.hughchou.org/calc/rdur.cgi

You will need to know:

- the beginning principle amount (the net proceeds from the house),
- the interest to be earned when you invest the money,
- an estimate of inflation and,

- how long you want to draw on the investment.

Try adjusting the figures for some different pictures. Shift your age brackets. Compute the dollars from age 70 to 100 (30 years), or from age 85 to 100 (15 years). If you wait until you are older, the chances are greater that you will want assisted living when you move in. (Assisted living averages about $1000 more per month than independent.) If you move in at a younger age, the reduction in stress may result in your not needing assisted services until a few years later. From observing your friends and family, could you agree that lowered stress might increase life span? Look at your genealogy. The same-sex relative you most resemble is still the best prediction factor for your life.

Factor in this information: For the comfortably retired in Denver in 2006, independent living for a single resident was as much as $3000 per month. Add $500 for the second person. Assisted living could be over $4000. Nationally, the cost-of-living in Denver is not as high as it is on either coast, but it is higher than in the midwest or south. With these variations in mind, you may need to consider selecting your retirement home in an area where you can get more for your money.

At this point you know that you have either (a) enough to live just about anywhere and also travel occasionally too, (b) enough to give resort living real consideration only if you choose your location carefully, do some creative financing and pace yourself, or (c) less than you will need. Don't close the book yet. Your options have just begun.

If your finances still seem hopeless, you could try for low income status. In Colorado in 2006, this meant your income is less than $30,120 ($34,380 for a couple) for the year and is adjusted income after subtracting your medical expenses. You do not have to rid yourself of your stocks and bonds, or the proceeds from the sale of your house, to qualify as low income. You may invest your assets and claim only 2% interest as income. You only have to "spend down" your assets to almost zero if you enter a nursing home and expect Medicaid to cover your costs there. These are 2006 facts and figures and are revised yearly. If you can qualify, do not hesitate to visit subsidized retirement communities. You will be pleasantly surprised. Staff and residents are friendly. Newer buildings may have high speed internet in each apartment. Your social image will not suffer. (See chapter 12, *Low Income Resorts*)

For those somewhere in-between, which includes many of us, there is no financial aid. Look at smaller residences that are independent but may have optional meals, perhaps a resident manager, and which allow you to bring in outside help as needed. This option enables you to hire assistance as you need it at reasonable prices. (See chapter 13, *Middle Range Resorts*)

Now that you know where the money is coming from, and how much, you can move forward in your planning.

11A. MONEY WORKSHEET

Source of $$$	2 People	1st Person	2nd Person
Social Security:			
Pension #1:			
Pension #2:			
Other monthly income:			
Total monthly income:			

Investment account #1:
Investment account #2:
Sale of house:
Sale of 2nd house?:
Other assets
Total value of assets:

From your total value of assets figure(s), determine how much of your assets could be drawn per month for the remainder of your years. Assume each person lives to age 100 for now.

Add your monthly income to your monthly draw and you have your estimated monthly allowance for resort living.

Compute several options for age-at-move-in date and length-of-life. Save this worksheet for future reference.

Examples:

age 80 to 100	=	20 yrs.
assets divided by 20	=	yearly assets
yearly assets divided by 12 months	=	monthly draw on assets
monthly draw on assets added to monthly income	=	allowance/month for 20 years

age 70 to 100	=	30 yrs.
assets divided by 30	=	yearly assets
yearly assets divided by 12 months	=	monthly draw on assets
monthly draw on assets added to monthly income	=	allowance/month for 30 years

You could plan to expend all assets at the higher end resort level and then move to subsidized housing when you qualify. See this example:

age 80 to 90	=	10 years
assets divided by 10	=	yearly assets
yearly assets divided by 12 months	=	monthly draw on assets
monthly draw on assets added to monthly income	=	allowance for 10 years

At age 87, get on the wait list for subsidized housing. Communicate clearly about the fact that your funds are running out and approximately when.

At age 91, assets are expended, move to subsidized housing, go on Medicaid for nursing care when needed.

Low income residence qualifications: Your annual retirement income plus 2% interest on remaining assets invested must be less than $34,380 per couple (Denver in 2006). Contact your local goverment for the specifics in your area.

12. Low Income Resorts

WHAT IF THERE IS no way you can afford deluxe resort living? You are not out of the game. Low income residences in the community will be a pleasant eye opener. Look in your telephone book in the government section. Under Human Services or Health Department look for Aging and Adult Services. Contact your local city government for information on projects subsidized by the city, as well as those built and maintained by nonprofit organizations in the area.

One observation is that there may be more interaction within the lower income community than in higher end residences. Folks may be more involved in what is going on and how things are run. They may be less inclined to expect things to be done for them. Second, low income is not shabby. Newness helps, but management and resident effort (and a little money) keeps any building pleasant and livable.

Now for the technical part. When you are on a limited budget, you have to be smart. Learn about Housing and Urban Development (HUD) subsidized programs, such as Section 8 Project Based and Traveling Vouchers. It's complicated. There is no need to recreate governmental regulations here, but the following is a specific example that will make it easier if you should apply for residency in a subsidized residence. If you know a little, it helps when you have to learn a lot.

I'm using Eaton Senior Programs in Denver, Colorado as a representative example of a low income retirement community; Willow Glen and Eaton Terrace are two of their residences. These dollar figures were current as of Spring, 2006, and will give an idea of what figures you can expect.

Willow Glen (WG) is a tax credit property. This means private investors, along with the city agency, Lakewood Housing Authority, built the building. It is owned by Lakewood Housing Authority; the investors take a tax credit for their investment.

The minimum age requirement for residents at WG is 62. Maximum annual income in 2006 is $30,120 for a single person, $34,380 for two. Rents range from $344 to $712 for a one bedroom and from $574 to $896 for a two bedroom. There are four levels determined by household income. Utilities are paid by the resident (gas, electric, telephone and cable TV) and may be estimated at between $75 and $100 per month. Therefore, the minimum income for a single resident must be about $800 per month in order to allow for rent, utilities, groceries, and other living expenses. There must also be evidence that the resident is financially responsible and is not in trouble with the law.

After initial move-in, if a resident receives a windfall or takes a job after the first year, they may still qualify if their income does not exceed 140% times the initial qualifying income level (for example, $30,120 x 140% = $42,168 or $3514/month). If their income remains below this level, their rent will not be increased. If their income increases more than the allowed amount, they will be offered a rent contract at the appropriate income level.

Anyone with income less than $1400/month may also apply to the Low-income Energy Assistance Program (LEAP) for additional assistance in paying their gas utility bills. This is a federal program operated by the counties. You can find information on the Internet.

WG accepts Section 8 vouchers which are issued by the Housing Authority. These vouchers provide 60 -70% of a resident's rent. They must be used in the city or county where they were issued for the first year. After that they may be used anywhere in the United States; thus they are also called traveling vouchers. They leave the resident paying 30-40% of the rent. These vouchers are difficult to obtain because the housing authority accepts applications on only one or two days a year, which are not widely advertised. You have to inquire and be a little lucky.

Eaton Terrace (ET) is project based. It is HUD operated and subsidized by the City of Lakewood. It was built and is operated by the First

Baptist Church of Lakewood as their church project.

At ET the minimum age requirement is also 62. Utilities, basic cable, and local telephone are included in the rent. Because ET is subsidized, tenants pay 30% of their adjusted gross income (after deducting estimated medical and prescription costs) with no minimum required. Lakewood subsidizes the balance.

All tenants are expected to participate in the meals program at a minimum level of 24 meals per month at approximately $180. Therefore, in reality, the minimum income for a tenant must be at least $180 per month to cover meals plus there must be enough to cover medical expenses somehow. There must be some income, but it can be very low.

Eaton Senior Programs is the nonprofit organization that manages Eaton Terrace Residences, Eaton Terrace II Assisted Living Center, Roger Manor, and Willow Glen Senior Residences in Denver, Colorado. Their Wellspring Senior Foundation enhances the programs and services provided through grant writing, fundraising events, and donations. It is their safety net of fundraising.

If you should decide to apply to a subsidized housing complex, expect to be graciously interviewed and helped with all kinds of financial and personal issues. Take a friend for support. It makes the visit more social and you will have a confidant to compare notes with afterwards. There will be a waiting list. Get on it even if your mind is not made up. If you are called, you can always decline.

13. Middle Range Resorts

IF YOUR FINANCES ARE limited but not low enough for subsidized qualifications, you are in really good company. Most of us are in that situation and there are solutions. You just have to understand the system. Here is the big picture:

In the high-end resorts, you rent the whole package: landscaping, lovely complex, large layout, large staff, complete activities program, full restaurant facilities, and an assisted-living wing with registered nurses. It's a big place with lots of advertising.

Middle range is not so well publicized. They do not have big advertising budgets. You have to look for them. The complex dining room, lobby, and staff are smaller, and there is no formal assisted living. They are pretty inside. There is less to maintain. There is a dining room, but the menu choices are fewer, and the meals cost less.

Smaller means more intimate. You know your neighbors better. The management knows you better. More personalized consideration is available. They want you to stay because vacancy is expensive for them. There may be a resident manager which means there is an able-bodied person available 24-hours a day for emergency assistance. You do not pay extra for this convenience.

In middle-range resorts, care is more personalized. There are fewer rules and regulations. Most often this means you may hire assistance from the outside as you need it for reasonable cost. This is the key. You pay independent living rates which are lower. You can rent a studio which is smaller and less expensive. You can have physical therapy come to you. You can have home-health nurses come to you. You can have hospice come to you. It will take more effort from your guardian to hire these services when you need them, but the cost will be more affordable. Meanwhile you have the social outlet and safety-net of group living.

So, compute your monthly allowance using the money worksheet. Determine a couple of alternate plans. You could compute fewer years. You could live deluxe and then move to low income when you qualify. Then, start your shopping. If mid-range is your choice, check the residency catalogs, specifically the ones that show rates. The cost figures will tell you where to visit. Don't settle for shabby. Shop until you find one that pleases you, just as you would if you were buying a new house.

Don't let middle resources keep you living alone. Living alone is dangerous, and it may be lonely and depressing. The human is a social animal. You will live longer, and better in the company of others. In your own family or in your neighborhood, you have known of some stoic person aging alone, being grateful for a few moments of conversation or a thoughtful gift of food. Most humans need fellows to survive and thrive, or they may die of loneliness. Find a fellow mid-ranger and shop together. Find something affordable and start your new life adventure.

14. Budgeting for Resort Living

Don't budget too tightly. You do not want to be a financial prisoner of your own making. In your former life it was always a good idea to live comfortably within your means and it is true in retirement living also. It might be useful to make a one word list of the items below and compare residences for cost. There is a sample worksheet at the end of this chapter.

The following is a list of expenses you could expect with variations, depending on the residence.

- Monthly rent. Even if you choose a buy-in community, you still have a monthly fee, though it is likely to be less than comparable independent living rent.
- Utilities, including heat and air conditioning. Usually included in assisted, but not included in independent.

- Phone. Likely, maybe just long distance. You might use only a cell phone, but be sure you can get clear reception in the building.
- Cable television. Probably.
- Internet. Check for internet connection and what type. It may come packaged with phone or cable television.
- Meals. Assisted living usually includes meals. Independent living charges for meals individually, and you want it that way, as compared to use it or lose it plans. There will be a ticket to buy to obtain meals.
- Garage or parking space. This is included in some residences.
- Laundry. Could be coin-operated, though in assisted it is usually included and done for you.
- Insurance. Buy apartment insurance. It is very inexpensive and will save you from a big bill if you or one of your relatives or visitors accidentally causes a fire or flood. It can happen.
- Auto insurance if you still drive.
- Prescriptions.
- Health insurance.
- Clothing. Probably will be less than in your former life. Some residences have small closets.
- Entertainment. There will be opportunities to go out for live entertainment or restaurant meals, at your expense. You will want to go.
- Vacations and travel. In your early years you may still take a cruise or tour now and then or visit relatives.

- Income taxes.

You will leave the following costs behind when you move:

- Mortgage payments
- Home insurance and taxes (again, buy apartment insurance)
- Home maintenance, including painting, lawn service, and carpet cleaning
- Purchase and maintenance on large appliances, refrigerator, washer/dryer, dishwasher, water heater, furnace
- Heat and air conditioning costs (possibly, but more likely in assisted living)
- Auto payment, gas, and insurance for your car when you stop driving

When considering the difference in costs, you may wonder what you are buying.

- Room or apartment, clean and modern with handicap shower, and grab bars
- Housekeeping, including laundering of your linens, and cleaning of bathrooms
- Maintenance of your unit including its appliances
- Heat and air conditioning are usually included in assisted, though you may pay in independent
- Meals, usually optional in independent, and included in assisted
- Entertainment, both in-house and offsite, with some cost extra

- Social life accessibility
- Safety net — someone is keeping an eye on you (and on your spouse so you don't have to)
- Emergency call system
- Fire sprinkler system
- Landscaping, ambiance, and pleasant common areas
- Transportation to grocery stores, shopping, appointments and activities
- Parking if you want to drive, which may be underground at some residences
- Peace of mind without nagging worries about when you should make the move
- Your children's peace of mind as they know someone is taking care of you.

14A. BUDGET AND RESIDENCE COMPARISON WORKSHEET

Budget Item		Residence		
	#1	#2	#3	#4
Rent				
Utilities				
Phone				
Cable TV				
Internet				
Meals				
Garage				
Laundry				
Apartment insurance				
Auto insurance				
Prescriptions				
Health insurance				
Clothing allowance				
Entertainment				
Vacations				
Taxes on income and capital gains				

Keep your personal preferences list in mind as you compare budgets. (See Chapter 16, *Your Must-Haves.*)

C. RESIDENTIAL
RESORT RESEARCH

15. Choosing Location

LOCATION IS THE FIRST priority. You could just pick a delightful community and let the rest of your life adjust, but that is probably not the best approach. Because you won't want to move again and again, a first consideration is whom you want to be near at the end. It could be your daughter, son, guardian, or your church, or the neighborhood where where most of your family and friends live. If your outside contacts were to become less and less, whom would you want to be near? Who needs to be able to get to you quickly, and often?

Having selected a location, what is available in the proximity? Is there a full continuum-of-care facility that pleases you, or will you choose an independent or assisted community with a nursing home or small boarding facility nearby should you need additional care? Tour the residences thoroughly in this neighborhood of choice. New residences are being built almost everywhere. Know what is available and the pros and cons of each. Visit several times and arrange to have lunch. Talk with other residents. Ask what they like and don't like if they were to move in today. Take your time.

The final considerations for location should be support, sentimental, and optional choices. Are there stores, libraries, walking paths, and restaurants nearby, or is transportation available? Did you grow up in this neighborhood so it feels like home? Is the residence pleasing to the eye, both inside and out? Is the neighborhood safe from theft and assault? Is the building secure?

The location may become obvious or it may come down to an intuitive choice. If you are not buying in, you can always move.

16. Your Must-Haves

WHEN YOU BEGIN LOOKING at possible retirement communities, you need personal ground rules to guide your search. Otherwise you will be overwhelmed by multiple options with no idea how to evaluate them. This exercise helps you be mindful of your wants, needs, and feelings in preparation for a future time when you will not be as active as you are now.

Think back to times in your past when you lived in an apartment or in housing that was close to your neighbors. What did you like and dislike? Compare that housing to your present housing. What do you most value there?

What must you have to be happy? What will your activities and interests include to maintain your sense of self and your wholeness when your body becomes more lethargic? At approximately age 80, what will support your day-to-day spirit? Keep in mind that at age 80 (like at age 20) you will feel pretty competent. Your family may have some skepticism about your decisions but probably won't interfere. You will probably have your health. You will be most of your best adult self.

It is reasonable to predict your needing something different from what you have now but not so extreme that you feel regimented, forgotten, and categorized as insane, helpless, and put somewhere. You will want dignity, respect, control, pleasure, entertainment, companions, mental stimulation, inclusion, laughter, and love. You will want it all.

My husband, Jerry, regards any kind of group living with horror. He identifies with his house, his truck, his tools, and his space on this planet. He sees himself as a responsible property owner and citizen of our city, state, and country. Jerry retired from the military. Group living for him means barracks and base housing. There is no way he will go willingly to any kind of retirement community. Not now or ever. That's what he says. Well, he is a healthy age 73. Surely he could remember things about base housing that were not that bad. Hopefully, in time, he will realize that he needs to protect himself from loss of control in the years to come before some "do-gooder" decides he is incompetent and commits him. He does not want to be on the news as that crazy old codger who held the authorities off with a rifle. At least I hope not.

In contrast, I am happily involved in the process of defining a comfort level now that could be projected into the future. I have enjoyed apartment living in the past and know exactly what I will need in detail:

- I like a temperate climate with seasons. Colorado is fine.

- I like the northeast corner of a building because of the morning sun and afternoon shade.
- I need a view; don't put me at ground level. The top floor is my preference with no one stomping overhead.
- I have to have a balcony where I can sit outside.
- I like dirt to plant flowers in; patio boxes are a must.
- I love to be outside, but it is already easy to stay inside most of the day. Maybe a place where there is a path to walk.
- I need a program director to create things to do. It's hard work for me to do the scheduling. I like guided tours if they are not athletic feats.
- I don't cook because I don't want to do the planning and shopping it requires. I love eating someone else's cooking.
- I like to organize people. I need a resident advisory council to belong to.
- I love the theater, movies, and live music, but not smoky bars. Sometimes it is hard to hear.
- I don't walk as far as I used to. One mile satisfies me where five miles used to be good, so twenty years from now I may prefer to ride in a bus or be dropped off at the curb rather than walk across a parking lot or a couple of blocks to the library.
- I love to write. Just give me a reason to communicate with someone and my fingers are on the keyboard. It looks like I also need a computer.

- I used to like verbal debate, but now I'd rather it were not too aggressive, and prefer a more thoughtful discussion.
- I read fiction, lots of fiction (but not war stories). The authors need to be more than amateur.

It takes some pondering and observation to describe your sense of self in this world. What do you do that makes you feel real, alive, excited, or pleased. You will need something similar in your new life.

It is going to take days of observation to put what pleases you on paper, but you need a list so that when you look for a safe place to dwell, you do not unintentionally isolate yourself from what makes you real. If I like to read, books should be available and rotated frequently. Jerry loves his tools. If he should never see another power saw or a worktable with a vice, could he maintain who he is? Fortunately he also loves to play his piano which is a little more practical in an apartment setting. What if he moved to a place where music was not valued? What if they did not allow pianos for whatever reason? Space for a piano must be on his list. He also loves his computer and the Internet, thus he needs a high-speed cable Internet connection. He likes to talk and needs social outlets. His lists are usually parts for something he is building, not social needs, but he still needs to take the time to make this list.

We all want some variation of quiet home, good food and social contacts, but we will not be pleased by the same solution. Some of us want a golf course. Some of us dislike high-rise living. There are those who want a strong religious tone to the activities. Some enjoy living in the bustle of the city, and others want quiet away from the sound and smells of traffic. The interesting part is specifying what details of the solution must be there to make each of us comfortable and content. Just what do I want, and what do you want for the last years of life?

Start your own personal preferences list. Put a pad and pencil near your easy chair on on the kitchen table where you can jot down ideas as you think of them. This is a brainstorm exercise — one of those where you don't criticize your ideas, you just record them for future editing. One idea will suggest another. List what stirs your passion. What activities or surroundings are necessary for you to spiritually breathe?

Then, prioritize your list. Is the north exposure as important as having access to a library? As you consider and explore the idea of safety-net living in any of its dimensions, having a written list will help you maintain a better perspective on what it will take to meet your needs.

You must formalize your list and save it where you know where it is (and maybe where your children know where it is) or you will forget, lose control, and someone else will decide what you need. Lists have a way of getting lost. At the very end you will probably be in a nursing home convenient for them. That's as it should be. But, if they are involved in moving you earlier, at least be ready with some written documentation to take a stand for yourself.

Better yet, move yourself.

17. Finding &
Evaluating Residences

CHOOSING YOUR NEW HOME requires more careful consideration than what has been required in buying your past houses. While you may be quite independent when you move in, there is near certainty that the community will be your support system while you are there and, perhaps, to the end. It is human nature to avoid imagining future incapacitating events, but in this case, you need to prepare for unfortunate circumstances such as a broken bone or a stroke. Keep these possibilities in mind as you search, and ask at each facility you visit how such eventualities would be handled should you choose to live there.

The first residence you visit might be one that you have seen advertised in your area, or one that you have seen in your daily travels. Choose a big one that will give you an extensive tour and lunch. Let them act as your tudor for your initial study course. Call and make an appointment as you would with a realtor. While you are there, take your time, visit with residents, and ask questions. Show them this book. You are a serious customer and deserving of their time. Expect to be treated as a valued guest.

You have completed your first step, and I hope it was fun as well as informative. Hopefully, you are excited to see another one.

Every city has some government agency that provides information on senior residences. Check this Web site: www.eldercare.gov It will direct you to a local information source. From there, you can get referrals to other information publications and offices in your area. Call and ask for a publication that lists rental rates. Start a file where you can keep your notes and all the brochures and handouts for each residence. Your education has started.

Create a checklist that is as complete as possible for your personal use and keep adding to it as you gain insight. I have found I need two types. One is a complete list for each residence with all the details. I make copies of this one. The second is an abbreviated basics list that has all the residences on it. This is one reason it is a good idea to shop early for your residence because you need time to comparison shop.

In touring residences, there are some general topics that are most important:

Food is Number One

Tour and stay for lunch, at least once. This is the most important item. Meals need to be served on schedule, with menus posted. They should taste good and offer variety. The attitude of the cooks and wait staff should be friendly and flexible. There should be enough space in the dining room to have guests without making a big deal about it. This said, scheduled double seating for meals is necessary in many facilities, but my preference is that there be enough dining room space for everyone to eat at the same time. The dining room must be pleasant, as you will spend a lot of time there. It should smell fresh and clean. A meal ticket system is a plus so that if you go out for a meal, you won't also be paying for a meal at the residence.

Curb Appeal

Would you be proud to live here? How do the exteriors and grounds appeal to you? The entire complex should be well maintained and pleasing to your eye. Does the common lounge feel comfortable to you? Some seem too fussy, and some too sterile. Look for comfort. Check the furnishings in the common areas for ease of use for older folks, those who need to sit and get up with relative ease without fighting the upholstery. Cleanliness tells you about pride of ownership. Would you be proud to have your relatives use the restroom in the common area? Safety precautions should be obvious. Tight carpet that accommodates walkers and handrails in the halls and bathrooms are good examples. Are the common areas spaces which you might use, or are they designed to look good to younger relatives? However, when you live in one of these residences, if the rooms are full, your life will be full. If there is low occupancy, management will cut costs, such as the budget for staff and food. Maybe the place should look appealing to younger relatives. They shop with their elders.

STAFF ATTITUDE

Someone will give you the sales pitch and a tour around the complex. Don't just turn this person off. Pay attention to how you are respected. Note if you are treated graciously or given a hard sell. Do other staff members speak and introduce themselves? Does the staff talk to your daughter or son more than to you, the future resident. You want to be treated like future family (you, not your son or daughter) and know that your needs and feelings are going to be important. You want to be adopted into a friendly group that interacts. You do not want to hear the staff talking about their dates or families as if you were not there. You want to be included in the conversations as if you were their mom or dad and you have an ongoing relationship. And you want them to act as if you might be the employer and that they are there for you, not you for them. You may have to live with these people twenty-four hours a day and you want to like them. Be sure you drop in on the residence you are seriously considering several times to evaluate staff attitude.

Residents

What do the residents look like and what are they doing? Are they your age? Listen. Does the place sound friendly? Sometimes if you drop in after lunch it seems like it must be nap time, and no one is around. My favorite residence always has a little background music, but you can also hear voices, kind of a friendly hum, folks picking up their mail, talking in the library or at the desk. Some afternoons there are five tables of bridge in the game room. What are residents wearing? Is this a dress-up place or are slippers and housecoats visible? Is there a beauty salon on site that serves both men and women? Again, would you be proud to have your family visit this place?

Money and Rules

Don't let the discussions of admission costs, termination issues and discharge rules get rushed past you. On your checklist there should be a clear space for deposits (refundable or not), rent, fees, and house rules. Get copies of their handouts and go home to fill out your checklist. Go back and clarify what you did not understand the first time. Do not let them rush you with promises of a room that is available today but will be gone tomorrow. If this room is really a must-decide deal, then get out that list and put your head together with your daughter or friend and be sure you understand all of it. Termination happens under many circumstances. If you are buying in with thousands of dollars, how do you get your value back, and how much, and when? If it is a rent situation, you need to know under what conditions you can move out and what penalties could be charged. If you are obstreperous, do they have to give you warnings? If you become incapable of taking care of yourself because of illness or a fall, can they evict you overnight? You need to know. Could your son or daughter move you out against your wishes? Under what circumstances? You were not born yesterday and you have learned how to deal with contracts in your lifetime. Don't throw caution to the wind now. Business is business.

RESIDENT COUNCIL

Be sure they have one and that it meets. Who are the current representatives and how are they chosen? What staff meets with them? What are the grievance policies and how do you make your voice heard without being obnoxious? This residence will be your community, and you need to know how it operates.

PRIVACY AND SECURITY

How is it enforced and respected? You may not have lived in a group setting since college, if ever, and you need to know how this residence makes it work. Do residents typically lock their apartments or rooms or is an open door policy in effect? What is the security plan? Do outside contractors come in to perform services and how do they gain admittance? Do you give them the door code or is there a receptionist? Staff should always knock and announce themselves before entering your rooms.

SMOKING

There will be a policy with specific smoking areas. Is it enforced? What happens to those who choose to violate it?

ACTIVITIES

Larger complexes will have an activities director on staff. There will be a regularly printed calendar of planned events. As a prospective resident, you should receive a copy of the current week or month in your information packet. Look at it critically. Is it all bingo, card games, and trips to the grocery store, or are there offsite events to attend. Would outside entertainment events be important to you? Ask a resident how often events are canceled.

APPROPRIATENESS

Finally, you like the place but does it fit with your personal choices list? What levels of service are offered and are they ones you expect to need? What activities are planned and do they fit your interests? There is no point in enrolling in the wrong class.

17a. Combination checklist

Location, Personal Must-Haves, Residential Evaluation
This checklist is a model of the three ideas that should come together in your evaluation. Your own will have these items on it and others that are important to you.

Location:

You need to be close to _____ so the location should be _____

Alternate location:

Personal Must-Haves by priority:

1. Outside contractors allowed (if this is important to you).

2.

3.

4.

5.

6.

Evaluation of Residences:

	Res. 1	Res. 2	Res. 3
Food			
Curb appeal			
Staff attitude			
Other residents			
Money and rules			
Resident council			
Privacy and security			
Smoking			
Appropriate for you			
Intuitive choice			

D. Making Your Move

18. What Goes With You?

THE OLDER YOU ARE, the more you need to be prepared for a sudden move. This is really important. When an unexpected event puts you down — the fall, the illness, whatever it is — very often you do not get an opportunity to return to your home. You never see it again.

At age 92 my mother-in-law went into dementia in South Carolina. She was transferred to a hospital, came back to her home for a mere week, and then we moved her to an assisted-living apartment in Colorado. In a state of confusion, she packed a suitcase with a few very worn outfits, some sheets and towels, and not much else. We retrieved pictures of family and her favorite tablecloth, her china, a few other things as we cleaned out her house. It happened so fast. After the move, she must have spent nighttime hours remembering her home and its familiar furnishings. What else could we do? We had to get her into a safe environment and get back to our jobs 3000 miles away.

She and I should have had a conversation early in our relationship. I was her only daughter, wife of her only son. I heard her say, "Jerry I am so tired," when she was about 85. At about age 88 she said she was getting so tired of all of her possessions. No, she would not consider moving to Colorado. I might have begun asking her what things in her home were most important to her, or she might have told me. But we did not know to do this, and we shared nothing. Jerry and I are loving children, but when the circumstances forced us to make decisions about getting rid of years of accumulated household goods, we had to take action.

As an elder, you need to give this probable progression of events more thought and be sure the things you want to live with come with you. Try standing in your living room and seeing all the unimportant things surrounding a few items you have emotional attachment for. How are you going to end up with what you want and leave the discards behind?

Cleaning out the stuff:

1. Get rid of clothing, shoes, and outerwear you don't like and that don't fit. Keep what you want to wear. Under duress, the children will choose the items in your closets that still look new, and the old ones will be gone. Well, the reason some things look new is that they don't fit or you don't like them so they don't get worn. The worn ones you love will go out. Your family can't make bad choices

in closets full of what you like. Every day think that if something were to happen today, would I end up with clothing I want and can fit into? Box up the rest in case you want to retrieve it later, and put it in storage.

2. Choose the furniture for your new smaller home. The big, worn pieces have to go. You may want all new furnishings for your small space. Keep only what will fit in a little apartment. If you need a new bed, help to buy the mattress yourself. Think soft. Your children will look at that old mattress that fits your tired bones so well and toss it, presenting you with a new firm twin that you can fall off of in one turn. Be sure you can get in bed without a step stool. Have you seen the height of mattresses these days?

3. Put your children's names on items they will inherit. Ask them if they really want it. Have them come over, load it, and take it away.

4. Plan to take very little from your kitchen unless you will prepare your own meals. Breakfast dishes, toaster, ice cream scoop, pie server, and a few decorations are all you need. You may have coffee and dessert for a couple of friends in your apartment, but no more big gatherings. They will happen in the small family dining room at the residence, and someone else will cook, serve and clean up. Terrific! If your heart breaks at the thought of never cooking again, I want to tell you about the last time my mother served us supper on her lovely china — her hands shook so badly when she passed the cups of coffee that

we knew this might be our last meal of her creation. She was exhausted. It is very possible that you will not have the strength to prepare and serve. Follow the advice I gave the men and envision yourself being the supervisor of the staff serving the meal and learn to enjoy.

5. Imagine life in an apartment. What hobbies, interests, or pastimes will work in a small space? Computers, music collections, books, video collections, musical instruments, crafts, and small tools are all good choices. What pastimes are you not getting around to doing anymore? Realistically, how long has it been since you used that sewing machine, table saw, or food processor? Would they be useful if you were living permanently on a cruise ship?

6. Label or list photo albums, wall hangings, and sentimental room decorations so that they are not forgotten. Add notes for historical detail, for example: "This glass sugar bowl was my grandmother's and was given to me as a wedding present." At the very least, someone will find the note and realize I did not buy the sugar bowl at a thrift store. Let your children know that such a list exists and take time, when appropriate, to talk with them about family treasures. One of my editors related that her husband's family had videos of their mother explaining her treasures and giving the history of each. They not only had the information, but the gift of their mother laughing and talking.

Talk with residence managers and marketing directors to locate the names and phone numbers of moving companies that specialize in elder services. Be sure to check their references.

Be prepared. Look forward, not back. Think adventure, cruise, resort. Move to your future, not away from your former self.

Go for it!

19. REALITY OF
A LAST RESORT

WHAT WILL IT FEEL like living in an old folks home? That's what it is. Think of all those old faces and bent bodies inching along the hallways. Walkers everywhere. Can you do this? Can it be home?

I'm going to move you in as an example of what it might feel like to start a new life in independent living. Since you have been planning this move for months or years, this is not an emergency move and you are emotionally prepared. Your attitude could be very different if you were not physically and emotionally ready for the change.

This is your first morning in your new place. You slept pretty well since you were really tired, but you were aware of sounds through the night. It is definitely going to be apartment living. There was far less traffic noise than at your house. You heard neighborhood dogs barking.

It seems easiest to maintain your old rituals, so you dress before eating a cold cereal breakfast. You could have gone down to the dining room for a continental breakfast, and you may start doing that.

You have always used a month-at-a-glance calendar. Over breakfast you compare the activities sheet for the residence with your calendar and began to fill in times and events. This morning at 10:00 is the weekly residence planning session. You have choir practice on Wednesdays, several previously scheduled doctor appointments, and an eight-day tour later on this month. You are still driving and you rented one of the garages. Someday you will have to schedule transportation. There is also a housekeeping schedule to post. The calendar is more full than ever. Your doorbell rings at 9:30. It is the hospitality chairman inviting you to the planning session. You thank her for the reminder. No more quiet days of solitude. Maybe being included isn't too bad.

You spend the morning at the planning meeting, noting the events that need prior sign up, and locate your mailbox and your other message cubby. You see the nurse in the lobby and she reintroduces herself. At noon you go to the dining room for lunch and take a table for two. You look around at your fellow residents. About a quarter use walkers. Some are members of your church. It is nice to see familiar faces and be greeted by former acquaintances. None are your close friends. You order the special and then desert. You give your new meal ticket to the waitress to be punched.

There is a movie after lunch but you are not settled enough to want entertainment. You elect to walk around the building for a bit of air and then to go back to getting organized.

A fellow church member stops by the apartment mid-afternoon and you chat. She invites you to join her for dinner in the dining room, and you accept. Later, another couple, who live down the hall, stop in and talk for awhile. They are not old, but they don't look like they still play tennis. Well, you don't either. They attend the tai chi classes. You might start that up again. They invite you to go to church with them. You try to remember their names. You need to start a roster of new acquaintances.

Just before dinner your older son drops in and you invite him to stay for supper. He declines but promises to bring his wife for brunch on Sunday. You talk him into coming for church before brunch. (Bribe the children when all else fails.) You walk with him down to the lobby where you meet your dinner date. She moved here about a year ago. You enjoy her conversation and eat too much. It is so easy to do. You decide to enjoy your own patio this evening and go to bed early. Your new TV will be delivered tomorrow. Your sister calls long distance to wish you well. No e-mail as your computer is not yet plugged in.

So here you are, your first day in independent living. It is not too different from living in your house. Casual conversation with others is closer at hand. Meals could be in your apartment or in the dining room. The library is four blocks away and the grocery about six blocks. There is a hardware store practically across the street.

You have made a calculated decision. You like this building. It is in a familiar neighborhood. There is an assisted-living floor, but there is no overnight caregiver.

There is a nursing wing available at a sister complex a couple of miles away. You know that if you need special care, you will have to modify your plan. This is your choice. You think you will be comfortable here. So far so good.

Note: Some of my readers have said this is far too hopelessly optimistic. It is my philosophy that you will find what you expect to find, and if you have done your homework in choosing a facility, you should not be unpleasantly surprised. This is apartment living and there will be differences, but generally they will not be unbearable. If there are real problems, such as noisy neighbors, take proper action with the management to resolve the problem, just as you would in any apartment situation. Make every attempt to maintain good relationships with all concerned.

20. Choose Your Guardian

REMEMBER OUR DEFINITION OF elder: a senior who requires some assistance. When you become an elder, you need a gofer – a runner, an errand person, a social secretary. You need a contact person with the outside world who has the energy that you do not.

While you are married, you don't need a guardian. Your spouse is your guardian. However, if you and your spouse are near the same age, you might want to select a younger person to advise you both and act as your representative on occasion. I expect that for gay and lesbian couples marriage will eventually be legal. In the meantime guardianship must be specifically acquired with the appropriate legal documents. You know more about this than I could begin to include. I'm going to talk spouse – you know what I mean. However, when that spouse or partner is no longer living, or if you have always been single, you need a legal guardian.

For an elder, a guardian is your second set of hands, feet and brain, a representative to accomplish your needs from basic purchasing of clothing to managing your money and signing contracts for your residence. Your guardian is your physical and legal self, thus the responsibility of guardian must be legally documented.

In the beginning, it can be as simple as someone on your signature card at the bank so that your money is available if, suddenly, you could not sign a check. However, you need to know that once signed, that account is owned jointly. I learned only in the process of being executor for my mother's estate that, by being on the signature card, her money was legally mine. In all of the years I had been her guardian, I had never thought of it as such, and had never signed my name alone but had always signed my mother's name followed by mine as P.O.A. (Power of Attorney). When I learned the account was technically mine, I felt uncomfortable, as if I had kept a secret from my sisters.

Choosing a guardian is a major decision for both of you. This person will be the keeper of your legal papers and will control the end of your life. On a "clear day" give it some careful thought. Who of all of your relatives and friends would be the best person to carry out your wishes when you cannot speak for yourself? Whom can be trusted with money not their own? Who has tact when the situation becomes stressful? Whom do you confide in about intimate subjects like illness, sadness, fears, religion, and end-of-life preferences? Whom can you disagree with and still maintain communication? Who makes decisions carefully but firmly? Who can handle the rest of your family if disagreement occurs? Who is most in agreement with you or will set aside differences and defer to your wishes?

Is there a natural leader in your family that fills this role, or will it have to be an unbiased outsider? This person will also rummage through your drawers and closet, comb your hair, take you to appointments, and help with clearing out junk mail and paying bills. This is the role of personal secretary in its most personal sense.

If this person is retired he or she might have more time to devote to you. This person needs to be younger than you so that he or she lives longer and has the extra energy to devote to your care. You could sweeten the responsibility by taking the two of you on travel trips or to local entertainment now and then, but it is probably not necessary.

In our experience, Jerry was the natural guardian for his mother as her only heir. I was the oldest of three sisters and our mother's legal guardian. I shared the responsibility for my aunt with her grandson. I was her personal secretary. He was our legal advisor and completed her estate after her death. He and I had not met until we accepted this responsibility and we worked well together. We seemed to have the same philosophy about her care, wanting only what made her secure and happy. It would have been difficult if one of us had been generous and the other stingy.

Giving this degree of trust is a risky act of faith. You need to know this person well. Take some time to make your choice. Here are a few illustrations about children as guardians and caregivers that will give you pause.

A friend of mine moved her mother and her paternal aunt in together into her very nice basement walk-in. However, the two old women had nothing in common. They endured quietly, seemingly gratefully. One loved TV, the other preferred the quiet. When the quiet mother passed on, the social aunt lived alone without anyone to communicate with except when her niece came home in the evenings. Her best hour of the week was when her niece took her to church. The aunt and I sat on a back pew and talked and I learned of her situation. My friend meant well, but was this the best situation for two elderly women? Enrolling the aunt in a day care center might have helped, but I did not know to suggest this option at that time.

While I was teaching my Last Resorts class, I met a friend of one of our church members at a local assisted-living community. She was a new resident, clearly a bit confused, but her face and manner indicated she was learning the ropes and enjoying her new life. Two weeks later I learned that her son had moved her. No one knew where she was, but he had determined that the residence was too expensive. Well, let's be fair. I am getting this information third hand and there could be many issues untold. However, the story illustrates the issue of vested interest. Our children will inherit all that we do not spend. Many will want the best for us no matter the cost, while others will openly or quietly resent or prevent our living in apparent luxury on their future inheritance.

I met a lady who had taken care of her mother and her aunt in her own home. Her siblings were not convinced she did it out of sincere compassion for her elders. When I talked with this lady, however, she described holding her mother in an embrace and reading to her for hours in her last few months. This description sounded like a sincere daughter's love. Was she manipulating the situation for some personal gain? I have no idea.

I know of an elder man who is cared for by his daughter and son-in-law. I believe his income is welcome in their household. The family culture is rather strict. He is disciplined more like a child than an elder. His misdeeds are reported openly to visitors. As he and I hunched together at the table over coffee, he told me he had lived too long but what choice did a person have? His eyes teared. Would he be happier with other elders in a group home? Maybe. The choice is out of his hands.

While you have the power, choose a guardian, and consider both your preferences and goals, as well as his or her personal needs. They should not be in conflict.

Empower your guardian. See an attorney who specializes in elder law, perhaps with your guardian. Your first appointment could be a free consultation. This attorney will point out issues for your consideration as well as identify the documents you need and what they authorize. He will have some interesting advice. Take whatever documents that you already have with you. If you have a Will and a Living Will, they may be adequate and only need to be on file. If you have a Health Power of Attorney and a Durable Power of Attorney, they may only need to be updated to include your guardian.

Conversations with your guardian need to be specific. Your guardian knows you and loves you, so most of what is done will be done in terms of being kind to an old friend. However, there are some subjects that need to be decided upon:

- **Residence.** How long do you want to stay in your home? Where would you consider living, perhaps in a retirement community? Are those communities conveniently located for your guardian since there will be numerous visits both necessary and for pleasure. Visit several together to compare what each of you sees as advantages and disadvantages. If you prefer to age at home, who might be considered as hands-on caregivers, assuming the guardian will not do it personally?

- **End-of-life Preferences.** Have several conversations about what life might look like in the end. I have a friend who wants to experience all of it, down to the last breath. As his guardian, which I am not, I would have to take that information literally unless he were to clarify it further. What if there were discomfort, lack of awareness? How about feeding tubes or ventilators? If you talk in terms of being kept comfortable and loved, it is not as morbid as if the conversation is just about when to pull the plug.

- **Relatives and connections.** If this guardian is not a relative, a list of relatives will be needed. Also, if the guardian is not a relative, make a list of who needs to be notified of the assigned responsibility, and what it includes. Are you connected to a church home, and who should be contacted about change of address or of your death? Do you want a memorial service, where, what kind, who should be included? You might consider writing an outline of your memorial service, choosing your favorite music, poems, readings, etc.

- **The money.** How much is there and how do you want it spent? When and how do you plan to sell your residence? When do you want your investments made available and how? Do you have an investment advisor or should you and your guardian visit one together? Do you need any security arrangements in place or do you have complete faith in your guardian? If your guardian has Durable Power of Attorney, all of these matters are legally his or hers to perform.

- **Be sure your guardian is spending YOUR money on your care.** Talk it over specifically. Very frequently in today's caregiving, an elder's costs are covered by the guardian's personal funds. It starts out innocently and becomes monstrous. Children mortgage their homes and cash in their savings to care for a parent. In the end, when it is necessary for you to move into a nursing home, funds remain in your account in excess of the minimal amount required for spending down, and Medicaid will not cover your nursing costs. Then the guardian is further compromised. Insist that your guardian charge everything on your credit card and pay the statement at month's end out of your accounts. Yes, you will spend down your assets. You must if your income is inadequate. Your government has programs to assist the elderly which were put in place to protect your family's financial well being. See that your children do not sacrifice their own futures on your elderhood.

Having chosen a guardian, have faith that your wishes will be followed as closely as possible and be at peace. You are in good hands.

20A. Personal Information Worksheet

Your guardian will need the following information:

Your doctor(s), name(s) and phone number(s)

Your dentist, name and phone number

Your bank, address and account number(s)

Locations of your checkbook, your driver's license, your Social Security card, and your health insurance card.

The owner name, address, and account number on your pension fund(s).

A complete list of your other accounts and investments.

Your church and the minister's name and number.

Your address book. Mark the friends you want to stay in touch with. Which ones are your best friends? Your favorite neighbors?

Location of your list of Must-Haves for residence choosing.

Location of your emergency hospital bag or box.

Location of your emergency nursing home bag or box.

Have you discussed your wishes about dying? Is it in writing? *The Five Wishes* form is a legal document in Colorado and may also be in your state.

21. If Everything Goes Wrong

YOU HAVE LEFT YOUR home, it is sold. The money is invested. You have moved into an independent living residence. Nothing has turned out as you had expected:

- You don't like the people.
- The food is lousy.
- The place is noisy at night.
- The staff attitude is snotty.
- There is nothing to do.
- Your spouse is furious.
- Your investments are dwindling.
- Somebody dented your car.

Remember, you are renting. You can leave. Are you making a judgment too soon? Give it a little time. Set a date for the decision in a couple of months. While you are waiting, start your search over again. Edit your list of preferences. Did you leave some important items out? Perhaps you are wiser now and would choose differently.

Maybe you are too young for retirement living. Perhaps an apartment for a few years would be better. Perhaps a residence with independent cottages would suit you.

Talk with your friends. What are they doing? Is there something you could initiate at the residence that would be good for you and others too?

It's not the end of the world. Don't panic. Take a little time to remake your decision.

E. SENIOR SURVIVAL

22. Curb Appeal for Seniors

Maintain your image, your curb appeal.

Seniors need to be extra aware of how they look to others. When a senior dresses down, wears soiled or very old clothing, combines odd colors, wears shabby shoes, or needs a haircut or trip to the beauty salon, that person is considered by the general public to be less intelligent or possibly deranged, but certainly no longer competent. No one will listen to your ideas or expect you to listen to theirs. This truth can make a great difference in your end-of-life years.

My dad had a bridge that filled the space of a missing tooth. When he would forget to wear that tooth, he looked like a vagrant. Add that to the dandruff on the shoulders of his yellow cotton jumpsuit combined with mail order canvas shoes and he was a bit pathetic. On the other hand, when he dressed well, wore his tooth, and had a fresh haircut, he looked distinguished and professorial.

Part of the problem is that we do not see as well as we used to. If a blouse or shirt is getting shabby or has stains, we do not see them. I have a tee shirt with daisies all over it including the back and sleeves. It is unique. It has been unique for years. The neckline is shapeless and the daisies are cracking but it remains in it's original state in my mind. I love it, but it either has to become a camping shirt or get pitched. Actually, why look grubby even when camping?

Pay attention to your table manners. We taught this to our kids. Take small bites. Eat quietly. Older jaws may not mesh smoothly so take your time. Chew with your lips closed. Remember to swallow before talking. Watch out for dribbles. Use your napkin often. My aunt suffered from Parkinson's so her fork shook. She wore clothes that required dry cleaning so spills were expensive. She did not have the dexterity to stuff her napkin into her neckline. We found a dentist's clip for her, the one with alligators at each end of a string. She had someone clip her napkin over her in front like a bib. It didn't look ugly, just practical. We had to remind her not to wear it away from the table.

How you are treated in the world affects your self-esteem but being mistreated can be largely your fault. You bring it on yourself with careless grooming. Apply makeup carefully, not too much. Comb your hair neatly. Older skin gets dry and cracked and needs lotion frequently. Nails get broken, and polish chipped. Make a regular appointment with the salon. Men, you too. Haircuts and manicures are little pleasures. These wonderful people will also trim your toe nails. How did those toes get to be so far way?

Hang a full length mirror near your front door where you can check yourself just before leaving — with your glasses on. Your fly is zipped. The tail of your belt is tucked into a loop and not left hanging. Your hemline is not tucked into your waistband in back. Your slacks are not hiked up by a sock. Do your socks match? Do your shoes match? Not everyone has the same color combination preferences, but give color a thought. Be self-critical.

You also need a mirror in the bathroom where you can see the back of your head. When we catch a quick nap in the afternoon, it is really easy to go out with a "sleep spot" where your hair is mashed bald in the back. No one will tell you, but everyone will notice.

Buy clothes that fit. If you shop the secondhand stores, great, but wear your glasses and try things on rather than just hoping they will become you. Look for newness and better quality. Be sure colors match and that there is still plenty of fresh life left in the cloth.

Even if you have played down your image as not important most of your life, now is the time to spruce up. Your appearance matters. Look good and you will receive more respect.

23. My Own Backseat Driver

I'VE NOTICED IT IS harder to keep my focus as I get older. You know that silly experience where you go the kitchen for something and can't remember what it was but you get a couple of things done there and then head for the bathroom. Usually you can remember why you are there. Then, as you wash your hands, you try to remember what it was a minute ago that you were going to do next. I have spent mornings getting nothing done but spending hours doing it. A list is my only solution.

In the same way, as I drive I find confusion at the edge of my thinking. Am I almost to the corner where I should turn, or is it a bit farther? Was I planning to stop at the grocery store first or second? Where is my former clear-thinking, efficient self? One answer seems to be talking to myself as I drive. I'm my own backseat driver:

"Let's see, check that list, everything together? OK, we're off."

There is no one there but me, but I talk as if there were more.

"Watch this corner, coming up. There are sometimes children in the street. Looks good. This next light is a long one. Good time to drink some water."

I'm especially helpful to myself on a highway:

"I think the center lane is the one we want. Check both the mirrors and a quick look over my shoulder. After that black truck, all clear, go for it. Good work. Next exit, stay in this lane."

As for my cell phone, if it rings I look for a pull off without even trying to answer it. It is so much safer to return the call than to juggle driving and phone answering.

So, if you see me driving along and my lips are moving, I'm not singing with the radio. I'm making sure I am thinking straight as I drive.

24. Pads and Other Personals

M Y MOTHER-IN-LAW DID NOT confide in me often. However, I was her only female contact and sometimes we did talk personal stuff. One afternoon we were sitting together in the assisted-living lounge. She was in her favorite space near one end of the long couch. She said she liked to sit here in the lounge, but sometimes it was hard to get to her apartment in time when she needed to use the bathroom. I put my head close to hers and said, "Emily, all of the ladies here wear pads. They won't ever tell you they do, but all of them do. I would be glad to buy some for you." She agreed to try them and that problem was solved.

Pads. They are high on the list of those "best inventions since...." They were perfected for babies to protect mothers' dresses and upholstered furniture. They have become so efficient that small children's spines are threatened when they carry around pounds of liquid in their pants. However, for seniors they are wonderful. No more embarrassing urgency moments.

My mother would stop suddenly as we walked down the hall and say, "Oh, I'm wetting my pants!" Then I would ask if she was wearing her pad, and yes, she was, and we walked on down the hall. She was safely protected.

In my Last Resort classes we had a special meeting for personal issues. We ladies met together, the men in a different room. I don't know what the men talked about but we ladies put a Poise® Ultra pad on the table and poured a pint of water into it. It held it all. Then we squeezed it and it still held. Miraculous.

Chuck confided to me that he had had to wear a pad since his prostate surgery. However, he had found Safeway's Guards for men are quite reliable and he was no longer afraid to drive for long distances or attend church functions for fear of an accident. Life picks back up and goes on.

Do you know about baby wipes? When you have a bit of a hemorrhoid and you have not just bathed, the itch is awful. No one wants to carry a wash cloth around with them, but baby wipes come in small, purse/pocket size packages, as well as a box size for the bathroom. They will save your bottom and your sanity. Of course, they are also useful for other cleanups.

Alcohol hand sanitizer will kill arm pit odor. Rub a dab in each arm pit and dry with a towel. If your clothing has also taken on that unfortunate odor, a little sanitizer in the underarm of your shirt will solve the problem until you can get home and change.

Have you tried liquid bandage? It is available both as a swab, and a spray. Our old skin resents having tape ripped off of it. The film that forms, when the liquid bandage dries, will hold and protect until you heal, even when it gets wet. Remember to take it on vacation, where scratches and cuts happen more frequently.

Older skin dries out and looks scaly, especially our hands and feet. Men, this is important, don't tune out. Try washing with Irish Spring® which loosens the dead skin, then rinse. Then use your wet wash cloth with no soap and rub firmly. It's easiest if you are in the tub rather than the shower. Rub your hands, feet, knees, elbows, wherever the skin rolls off. Rinse again. Dry yourself and apply lotion while your skin is damp. Every now and then give yourself this skin treatment, or at the very least, on your hands and feet.

Wheels are available for everything, such as suitcases, grocery dollies, garden carts and wagons, and briefcases. Load up your walker. Don't carry stuff, roll it.

About walkers: You need two kinds. One is that light aluminum folding walker that packs easily in the car and takes up very little space in a restaurant. Look for larger wheels, say six inches or so, that won't catch in elevator doorways or on the edge of carpets. The other is one with a hand-break and a seat. These are more awkward for packing in a car, but are best for all-day use. There are also pockets for things you want close at hand: tissues, pen and note pad, a small calendar, and your keys. Look for big wheels and hand break levers that are easy for frail hands to operate.

A Tai Chi instructor introduced the practice of, "oiling your joints" to his students to keep them occupied while he was giving long dissertations on the history of the sport. He said that if a joint is moved repetitively for a minute or so, it lubricates itself. You oil a joint by circling the body part below it lots of times, slowly. Open and close your hands for your finger muscles. For your wrists, move your hand in a circle like you would if you were mixing something in a bucket or bowl with just your hand, not your whole arm. Do it both clockwise and counterclockwise. For your elbow, turn an imaginary crank with your hand and forearm. Then backwards. For the shoulder, bend your arms and draw circles with your elbows, in both directions. Stir with your foot for your ankle joints. For the knees, hold one up at a time with the calf and foot dangling and swing the foot in a circle both ways. Your hip will move if you draw circles in the air with each knee in turn. You could try these joint exercises when you are waiting for the coffee to perk or for the skillet to get hot. Doing them in the supermarket line might look suspicious.

25. Use It or Lose It

MAINTAIN YOUR BODY WITH determination. Think of it as your vehicle and you are trapped inside. You cannot change the make or model from what you were "manufactured" with, but you can try to maintain what you have. This is my closing poem for retirement living:

Walk.
Sit straight and stand tall.
Get down on the floor and get up, every day.
Establish an exercise routine.
Rejoice in the health of your body.
Walk.
Drink water.
Manage your weight.
Eat variety and color.
Enjoy fresh air.
Walk.

Do new things.
Cultivate a few close friendships.
Talk on the phone.
Write letters and e-mail.
Walk.
Have your hearing checked.
Get an eye exam.
Know your blood pressure.
Take your vitamins.
Walk.
Nourish your skin — wash it, cream it.
Keep your hair styled and trimmed.
Manicure your nails.
Smile at everyone you meet.
Walk.

Part II

Nursing Homes

F. Perhaps,
A Nursing Home

26. Last Vestiges of Control

THERE'S NO WAY AROUND it. We need to know about nursing homes.

Someday your guardian and/or relatives will take care of you. It's not what you want but, eventually, you will need their help. If you are smart, you will have had discussions and spent time looking at various options. You will have put your heads together.

Many long-term care insurance agents have managed to frighten people into buying insurance against being poor and put in one of those horrible places. The nightmare of years and years in a nursing home fills our imaginations.

The truth is that unless you get so frail that you cannot walk, or feed yourself, or cannot get up if you fall, assisted living will probably meet your needs. Assistance in bathing, getting to meals, dressing and undressing, and grooming is normal. If you can walk without someone holding on to you, you can be pretty delusional and still stay out of nursing homes. A cane or walker as assistance is okay. Unless you have a stroke or serious fall and can't walk, you do not need to be in a nursing home – unless your family doesn't know any better and puts you there.

27. THE REALITY OF A NURSING HOME

WELL, IT COULDN'T LAST forever. You carefully plotted your retirement residence lifestyle and were enjoying it completely. Sure, you were slowing down a little, but still coping. Not down yet.

But then it happened – that simple little fall and you are out of control. It only takes a second. Then, there was a stay in the hospital and the doctor's pronouncement, "You will need ongoing care."

The indignity of it all. Your bag was packed by someone else, a family member whom you tried to tell which items you wanted. It is so hard to remember your wardrobe and which items will be useful now. Underwear, slippers. It is unbelievable. This is it, you have lost the power to run your own life.

Wheelchairs – they were always for someone else. Big, awkward, bumpy-riding things. You are rolled from a car, through big double doors into a carpeted room and parked near a reception desk. Pasty-complexioned people sit around the room, motionless, no one looking at you. There seem to be multitudes of people in varying uniforms flitting around, speaking in patronizing tones. Canned music, bells ringing, the slight smell of food from the last meal. A caregiver kneels down near a sleeping woman in a chair, "Mrs. Jones, may I give you your medications?"

Here she comes. The head nurse with a big smile and loud voice greets you with, "Don't you like our holiday decorations?" You are rolled down the hall and into a room with a very wide door. Twin hospital beds with a curtain between. The nurse rattles on: "You will share room 415 with Mrs. Palmer. Your half of the room is this right side away from the window. Here is your closet. You also have the right side of the cabinet in the bathroom. There are two telephones on a splitter; no long-distance calls. The TV has remote control. The wall on your side is yours to hang pictures. This is your side chair for guests. I'm sure you will be happy here." She is gone.

Your daughter is chattering at you, putting away your belongings where you will have to find them later. Heaven knows what she packed for you. Did she say something about marking your name in your clothes? Well, there is nothing left for her to do. She says, "Goodnight dear, sleep well, see you tomorrow, someone will be in to help you" and she is gone. Well. You sit there in your chair waiting to see what happens next.

A lady with stringy gray hair is rolled into the room by an aide in colorful scrubs and is introduced as your roommate, Mrs. Palmer. Like at the hospital, you have no choice in roommate. Hopefully her family is not too large or noisy. Mrs. Palmer is talking loudly to the aide who is rummaging in the closet. The aide sets the wheel lock on your chair and hands you your nightgown. You quietly dress for bed. You pull the blankets back and slowly get yourself into the bed, trying to be inconspicuous, wondering how to best cope. The lights go out, there is music in the hall, then all is quiet. You sleep fitfully in the strange surroundings, getting up once on shaky legs to find the bathroom.

An unfamiliar aide bursts into the room and opens the curtains to the daylight. She helps you decide what to wear and shows you where your toothbrush and toiletries have been stored. A male orderly comes in and offers to roll you to the dining room where you are pushed up to a table on one side of the room. A young waitress comes to the table and offers you a choice of breakfast menu items. Another resident is rolled to the opposite side of the table. She says she is Mrs. Stanley and she tries to start a conversation.

Well, you might as well cooperate, this is your new life.

28. Pack your own Parachute

IF YOU ARE NOT a "parachute packer," you may find this idea extreme. I'm going to do it, but you decide for yourself.

In advance of an emergency, I would recommend that we all prepare for this probable event by packing two bags, maybe not in a suitcase but in a well identified-drawer or box. The reason for these two bags is that when that episode happens, you may never see your home again. You will not pack bags or pick your clothing, but you will try to tell someone what you need and they will rummage through your closet and dresser. Embarrassing thought.

Bag one is for the hospital. You need pajamas (two piece sets seem to work better in the hospital), a robe, slippers that you can slip into without help from your hands, toothbrush and toothpaste, a hairbrush, lipstick or chap-stick, deodorant, incontinence pads (would you believe the hospitals don't seem to know what they are), and maybe a book (not hard cover, too heavy).

Medical cards, credit cards, and your various identifications will be in your purse or billfold which will probably be with you. Give it to your responsible relative as soon as possible as things disappear in hospitals.

Bag two is for the nursing home and is in addition to the contents of bag one which is already with you. You need washable, pull-on clothes, with pockets, that are mix and match (maybe ten sets, get them at the secondhand stores), plenty of underwear, shoes you can slip into (maybe velcro tennis shoes) and socks, a washable sweater or light weight jacket or vest, a container with a lid or zipper for toiletries, handkerchiefs, a couple more books, photo albums of your family, a couple of momentos you will love having with you, a couple of pictures to hang, and your stuffed animal. Mark your name on everything with permanent ink.

29. Coping in a Nursing Home

S O, HOW DO YOU keep your sanity and make the best of a nursing home? From my experiences with my relatives and their fellow residents, some of these methods may be useful:

Your space. Identify your territory. Where is your room in relation to the baths, dining room, and day room. Do you get a regular place at the table? Get a lay of the land and which parts of it are set aside for you. Is there a place in the day room where you feel most comfortable? If you can identify where you will be and when, you will feel less disoriented.

Time. Learn the schedule, which may be different on Saturdays and Sundays. The staff may also work four-day

weeks, so your helpers will be different but they will be
the same for several days in a row.

Rules. Observe how the rules apply. Do you use a
walker or wheelchair? Are you allowed to walk unassisted?
Are karate-style waist belts or wheelchair seat belts used to
prevent you from falling?

Hygiene. Decide how to best take care of your hygiene
in this setting. You will be on a bath and shampoo schedule
and it may not be at times you would expect to bathe.
However, you will receive help, so although changing
clothes in the middle of the day will be unusual, it will feel
good to be clean afterwards. They will shampoo your head
the first time whether your hairdo is destroyed or not and
they may not explain why. They are trying to prevent lice
and other communicable conditions. Go with the flow. So
much for modesty; your privacy is gone forever.

Belongings. Find a way to mark your clothing and
belongings (toothbrush, lipstick, chap stick, personal stuff),
maybe with colored electrician's tape. Your roommate may
not have the mental acuity to identify his/her toothbrush,
hairbrush, or chap stick from yours. Find a container to
hold your items easily and put them away together in a
bathroom cabinet. If your container has a lid, it may help
protect your personal items from being used. Your hearing
aids and dentures will mysteriously disappear if you do
not concentrate on putting them in a specific place. If you
have a relative who could take your soiled clothes home
and wash them, you may not lose so many items. Some

nursing homes are better than others at protecting your clothing from disappearing. Don't bring your expensive outfits; let your daughter keep them or give them away.

Staff. Which staff members are responsible for you? You will learn that you have regular nurses, regular caregivers, regular servers in the dining room, but they all have days off. Learn from whom you should ask for help, rather than just asking whoever happens to walk by. Who can take you to the bathroom or change the setting on your room's thermostat?

How can you connect with the staff for your safety and comfort? Establish a rapport; talk about family, both yours and theirs. Make personal friends just as you would if you were in a hospital for an extended stay. Be sure to find out who is the real decision-maker, who has authority.

Grooming. How do you take care of your grooming needs (shaving, hair styling, nails)? There will be some system of making and keeping appointments. If you keep yourself looking reasonably well groomed, you will receive better care and consideration from the staff. Really. And grooming is a diversion. Use it.

Diversions. Evaluate your needs, abilities, and remaining capabilities. You may not be able to be involved in crafts or using tools. Can you read, maybe large print books? Do you contact your family with e-mail? Do you listen to the radio, music, or news? Is there a window where you can sit and watch the outdoors, or maybe a patio to sit outside. Do you still enjoy TV – sports, drama, community programs? Look for ways to be creative: writing, painting, knitting, or service to others. Reach out in conversation. Helping others is good for you. Find ways to meet your needs.

Social contact. Watch the group for evidence of presence of mind. Some of these folks will seem rational at first but will turn out to be stuck in the same repetitive groove. Pacify them, but look for others. Reach out to those who might need conversation. Those folks asleep in their chairs may just be bored. Look for opportunities for diversion, such as excursions on the facility bus or outside entertainers coming in. Don't expect them all to be good. Stay in touch with the world. Find a corner where you can see outside.

Comfort. You may find a stuffed animal wonderful for emotional support, an outlet for affection. Big and comical is good. Don't hesitate to confide in your stuffed animal since you need someone who understands you intimately that you can hug in the night.

Family. Know that this is as hard on your family as it is on you. If there are real problems you need help with, ask. However, assure them that you are reasonably comfortable and receiving good care (if you are). Maintain as much relationship with family as you can for their sake as much as for yourself. This is the end of your history with them and you need to help write it.

30. Nursing Home Care is not Perfect

This chapter is mostly for the relative that is in the guardian role. Thank you. Your task is hard work. Perhaps these ideas will help.

CHOOSING A NURSING HOME is traumatic. You are placing your elder in the care of others in an institutional setting. The choice is often made in haste following a hospital stay. A social worker in the hospital may help. It is called "locating a bed," which sounds so uncaring. You will quickly discover from these efforts whether there is a shortage of beds or if a selection is available. You will definitely lose sleep over this process. Visit in advance if possible. Moving twice is not desirable. However, you do not sign a lease so change is not difficult if you find a home you like better later.

Carpeting is not as important as having adequate staff with a caring attitude. If the staff is gathered at the nursing station talking about last night's party, they are not talking about patient care, which is where their attention should be. Pay attention to the low level staff who push wheelchairs around and feed patients. Sense what their attitude is and whether you would be pleased to be served by them.

Your elder may live in the space you choose for the rest of their life so look at it from the elder's perspective. If he/she is comatose you just want comfort for hospice. A person who is sick/delusional needs a small space, not too bright or busy, a nest to curl up in. An alert and interactive elder needs a window onto a decent view (unless the bright light is a problem), comfortable looking surroundings, and activities and amenities that are appropriate for his/her interests.

Not all nursing homes are ugly, smelly, noisy, barren, miserable places to live and visit. Ask other visiting family members what they have experienced. Ask your friends who have cared for their parents. Take the time to check out enough locations that you can sense the difference. Do not hesitate to change your mind if, after you have made your choice, it becomes obvious that another home would suit your or your elder's needs better.

In a Medicare facility, all residents must be accepted. There are a reasons for choosing a private nursing home over one that accepts Medicare patients. When my mother was recovering in a lovely Medicare home, there were patients calling out, "Help, Help!" even though no assistance was needed. They might have been carrying on a conversation at the same time. I saw a resident grab a nurse's arm and she had to pry his fingers from her wrist. Craziness was accepted. At the same time, my mother-in-law was in a private nursing home. A resident yelled and threw food at lunch. By evening he did not live there anymore. Private facilities have total control over whether a patient stays or is refused service. If you compare the cost of private or Medicare, the difference is not too great, all things considered. However, since Medicare will pay for about six weeks of care after an accident, you may want to take advantage of that coverage, but when the period runs out, do not hesitate to move your elder to another facility.

On the other hand, no matter how they try, not everything can be done. It's not going to be flawless. It just needs to be enough.

The following are some helpful nursing home hints:

- **Incontinence.** Most brands of paper pants are good (smocked paper briefs with padded crotch). The patient can't put them down the toilet. They tear off on the sides but one leg of the slacks have to be removed to put on a new pair. I learned to do it. Many homes use adult diapers, like the infant kind, only sloppier. They are plastic covered and fasten with tape. These can be changed without removing the patient's slacks. They are more humiliating to the patient (and to you). It's really hard to keep elders' privates clean, and diaper rash is frequent. Baby wipes are a blessing; you should probably use the flushables. Twice a week showers are barely enough.

- **Clothes.** They get lost even if they are labeled with the patient's name. Don't take good clothing to the nursing home. It may be best to have the family do the laundry and have enough changes to accommodate twice-weekly laundry. You should check the lost-and-found in the nursing home laundry periodically just in case. Older folks like to dress warmly; turtle necks, cardigan sweaters, washable and no ironing needed, of course. Layering clothing works well. Shop secondhand stores. Buy only pretty, well-maintained items.

- **Comfort.** Elders appreciate a nap blanket which can be used during the day when lying on top of the made up bed. A couple of yards of polar fleece from the fabric store is great. Stuffed animals are also good snuggle objects, something to hug or put between the knees for comfort.

- **Slippers and shoes.** Slippers need to be easily stepped into, not too shapeless, with the elder's name marked on the bottom. Velcro-fastening tennis shoes with fairly smooth bottoms are practical for physical therapy sessions or going out with family. Mark Right and Left inside (a big R & L) where it is visible to the elder.

- **Pictures.** Big, color pictures bring a remembrance of family. Don't bother with frames. Big prints can be attached to the walls

around the bed with poster putty and moved or
added to easily. Put some in the bathroom too.
Be sure your elder can see well enough to enjoy
them, otherwise they are just a reminder of one
more failing sense.

- **Attention.** Call bells, patients crying out, staff
  conversations. It's a noisy place. Fortunately,
  most elders are partly deaf. A room away from
  the main drag is quieter but gets less walk-by
  attention. Putting out a dish of candy for the
  staff brings staff walk-ins. You don't want your
  elder ignored.
- **Staff conversation.** If they are chummy and
  joking together, the patients are being ignored.
  Conversation should be with the patients or
  about patient care. It is hard enough to keep the
  communication lines clear about who needs
  what, and current changes in care plan, without
  the distraction of socializing between caregivers.
- **Flexibility with family.** If you can drop in and
  share a meal with your elder, either bringing
  your own food or being served from the dining
  room, it is comforting to elder and family. You
  can check out the food and surroundings. In
  nursing care you probably will not be served
  in the patient dining room due to privacy and
  dignity issues for the other patients. However,
  there should be a place where you can be served
  with your elder.
- **Quiet visiting.** Places to sit both indoors and out
  with your elder need to be available. Just sitting

in the semiprivate room is uncomfortable for all
and the elder needs a change of scenery. Rocking
chairs on the porch are great!

- **The bathroom.** There is very little counter space
  near the sink for each resident. Initially you
  might try using the dishpan shaped plastic tub
  from the hospital for keeping personal items
  together in the bathroom. However, if your elder
  can manage a container with a lid or zipper, you
  might find one to keep personal items personal.
  Truthfully, there is no way that I have found
  to keep your elder's toothbrush and grooming
  items private. Delusional people use whatever is
  at hand, gross but a fact of life. Also, the toilet
  paper used is inexpensive. I like to substitute my
  favorite brand. (This personal items situation
  alone is good motivation to find a small group
  home with private half bath for your elder, if
  appropriate.)

- **Doctor's orders.** They may or may not be
  followed. It depends upon the staff assigned
  directly to your elder. If there is a large staff with
  diversified and rotating responsibility, orders get
  lost. Orders such as "keep a pillow between the
  knees when in bed" or "elevate the head" may
  not happen reliably. Prescriptions are probably
  given as directed. If there is a responsible
  caregiver for your elder, things like shortness of
  breath may be detected early; if there is a large
  staff, it may be noticed after a couple or three
  days. By visiting often, you may catch some of

these issues. Pick your battles, don't crab about everything or your voice will not be heard. Then again, pneumonia may still be the "old folks friend" when they wish to move on, since antibiotics are frequently no longer effective.

- **Phone.** One can be hooked up but elders may not have the mental focus to use one. If you install one, in an emergency your elder may be able to reach you. Even if clear communication is not possible, you will know something is wrong and physically check it out. However, elders may turn the receiver upside down, not be able to hear, or be unable to reach the phone. Staff does not always think to locate the phone within reaching distance. If your elder can manage a cell phone, keeping it in a pocket could be an answer, but recharging it may be a challenge.

- **Space.** Space within reach beside the bed is very limited. When you add tissues, phone, book, reading glasses, glass and pitcher of water, television remote and call button, and maybe a shoe horn to the already present table lamp, the space is a total clutter. If there is a hospital table in addition to the bedside table, it helps. If your elder uses a walker, some of these items could be in its pocket. However all of this may be out of reach if the elder is in bed. This would be a good problem to solve by invention. Hospital bedsides have the same problems.

- **Call button.** They are frequently beyond the comprehension of an elder, especially in an emergency. Many are combined with the TV to make matters more confusing. If elders really need help, they will usually call out verbally and may get out of bed to summon a nurse. Additionally, they have been going to the bathroom in the night by themselves all of their lives. There is no way to keep them from doing this short of tying them to the bed which few of us want to authorize. If a fall results from this situation, it is just one of the risks of life. We could not prevent this kind of accident if our elder was in our home unless we hovered over them twenty-four hours a day. Prevention may include having staff wake them periodically in the night for a bathroom visit, a solution that is not fail proof either. Old people fall. We just have to accept this possibility.

The hardest part of having your relative in a nursing home is absorbing the realization that they may hold steady for awhile, but in the long run they are not getting better and coming home. Any other time in family life, a person goes to a hospital and recovers. You hover and assist and be sure they are safe. Well, this time you can hover your heart out, wear yourself to a frazzle, and they will still die. Unless you are a real scrooge, your conscience is beating you up for not keeping them at home, close to you twenty-four hours a day, emotionally in your arms. It can't be helped. Try to set yourself a schedule based on the cognizance of your elder just as you would for a toddler.

Let the schedule of the facility support you and you pick up the slack.

For instance, if the resident schedule has breakfast and hygiene in the morning, don't get in the way. Show up for late morning, maybe for lunch or just until lunch, then maybe again before dinner or at bedtime. Talk about what your elder remembers, again and again and again. These are times if they were at home you would be chatting over coffee, telling what your plans are for tomorrow, tucking in for the night. Be part of the care staff on a regular basis, not an irregular interruption.

When conversing with a nursing home resident, try to speak with them just as you did when they were living at home. No baby talk, no extra terms of endearment. Give them credit for being adult even if they are delusional. I heard an aide arguing with a resident who was concerned because there were two children in her room. The aide said no children were there. The resident insisted there were. I took the aide aside and suggested that she tell the resident that she had, indeed, found two children in the room and had sent them downstairs where someone could watch after them. The wide-eyed aide gave it a try and the resident was easily pacified. Jerry's mom had visions of kittens playing on the floor near her wheelchair. When he came to visit she would tell him how cute they were and he responded that he was glad she had them to entertain her. He would ask how many were there today. The number would vary from three to five and the one with the white spot was her favorite. You know the fact that what the resident is seeing in not there, but it gives them peace of mind to be agreed with and not confronted. You are not making fun of them, you are taking their perception seriously. It is real for them.

Remember, this elder probably took care of you once, and is feeling more or less like an imposition on you and your busy life, but you are needed at the same time. So make it smooth, seemingly routine. "See you tomorrow, Mom."

G. Alternatives
to Nursing Homes

31. Total Longterm Care

Total Longterm Care (TLC) is not insurance you are buying for long-term care.

When you read this you will wish this package were available to you now, but it is for nursing-home eligible elders only, really frail folks. If you are caring for a failing spouse, this may be an answer.

Again, this program is total care outside of the nursing home for folks who are nursing home eligible. There are six basic daily living skills and the elder must have trouble with at least two of these skills: bathing, dressing, undressing, eating, transfer, and continence. Additionally, the elder could have mental incapacity.

TLC is part of the federal program called PACE (Program for All-inclusive Care for the Elderly). It is a nursing home alternative. The PACE program is national. If you are involved in caring for a parent long distance, this may be very important information.

Eligible individuals who wish to participate must voluntarily enroll. You cannot register your relative against his/her will.

PACE enrollees must also:

- Be at least 55 years of age.
- Live in the PACE service area, organized by zip code.
- Be screened by a team of doctors, nurses, and other health professionals as meeting that state's nursing facility level of care to determine if nursing home care is actually warranted.
- At the time of enrollment, be able to safely live in a community setting. If an elder should become a danger to self or others, PACE will relocate him/her to a Medicaid funded nursing facility. Nursing home residency is not avoided forever.

According to the PACE brochure, the plan "provides a family with all the support they need to keep their senior family member in good health and good spirits, in their own homes or communities, and out of a nursing home." Add "for as long as is possible."

The following **services** are included and available at or from the day-care center:

- All physician services (no appointments necessary)

- Dentistry, podiatry, optometry, Audiology (no appointments necessary)
- Hospitalization and emergency services
- Housing placements (nursing home if necessary)
- Prescriptions, both supply and monitoring
- Transportation (home to center and elsewhere if needed)
- Rehabilitation therapies and equipment
- In-home services: housekeeping and skilled care
- Social work services
- Adult day program with activities, socialization, and meals (retirement home advantages)
- Coordination of all services by a case manager.

Medicaid has determined that it is less expensive to provide all of these services in-home or at the day care center than to pay for residency in a nursing home. Most likely the elder is also happier. When nursing home residency cannot be avoided, that is also provided. You could not buy these services individually with any efficiency or coordination.

The entire program is covered for you if the usual Medicaid eligibility boundaries for income are met. In 2006, the maximum income was $1700 per month and assets less than $2000. An elder could pay privately, in the $3000 a month range, which is about half the cost of a nursing home. If the elder is staying in a residence that allows outside contractors to come in, TLC could apply.

Of course, there are qualifying decisions, cost evaluations, and huge family considerations. But if you are (or are caring for) that rugged individualist who won't leave home before age 95 if ever, TLC may be your best resource.

Check your government listing for PACE

Do not depend on this information remaining complete or up to date. Contact your local PACE office and verify all figures and qualifications: www.totallongtermcare.org

32. Another Nursing Home Alternative

CONSIDER A SMALL GROUP home or personal-care boarding home. After I found the most beautiful nursing home for my mom, I learned the misery of nursing homes.

The medical staff was superb. Doctors saw my mother regularly as her hip healed and she recovered from pneumonia. I was not always there when they were there, so communication was not smooth, but they did prescribe appropriate medications and treatments. The occupational therapy staff was very good to work with. They were kind and Mom felt they were on her side. The nursing staff was conscientious and personable. No problem there.

My problem was with the low level staff. Clothing disappeared in the laundry; I soon decided to do her washing myself. Patients were rolled into their rooms and left with wheelchairs facing the wall, nothing within reach. Gossipy conversations between staff helped them pass their working hours. Food was served as it would be to inmates. Kindness was absent. Added to the audible and visible mental health problems of other patients, this disrespect for elders motivated me to find another solution for my mother, and for me. I could not stand the situation.

A friend told me of the group home she had found for her dad. I visited and was immediately pleased. I took Mom there for lunch and a mini-tour. She quickly decided on the little furnished room with a nice window and she loved having her own half bath.

Small group homes and personal care boarding homes are private residences converted or built for the purpose of housing a small number of elders in an extended-family-like setting. There is usually a common-area great room including kitchen, dining area, and sitting room. Residents eat family style and are served home-cooked meals prepared by the staff. Each resident has a private room with closet and half bath. (Medicaid funded residents may share a room.) The showers and bathtubs are down the hall in a room that provides for supervised bathing and shaving. The staff may also shampoo and set ladies' hair and give haircuts for both sexes. There is a house laundry where each resident's clothing is kept separate, washed, dried, and folded. The staff creates appropriate activities for residents, including bingo, light entertainment, watching TV, nail painting for the ladies, and whatever else is needed. Someone is on duty twenty-four hours a day. Family visitors can come and go freely and may also be invited to stay for lunch.

This setting is ideal for the elder who needs only regular prescriptions (no IV's or catheters), constant supervision (does not wander), assistance with dressing and bathing, and just basic loving care 24 hours a day by semiprofessional homemakers.

This solution was perfect for my mother, who was often confused and could not initiate conversation or social interaction for herself. She was childlike but knew who she was and where she was. The house was my elder-sitter and I was there as my schedule allowed. Mom had a room she could call home and caregivers twenty-four hours to handle her physical needs and administer her prescriptions. It worked for us much better than a nursing home. We both needed the smaller setting.

Always get a recommendation from a former resident's family before placing a relative in a small group home. Visit unannounced. There are mercenaries in this business. I would also look for a building that was constructed originally for the purpose. Remodeled family homes may have stairs and be short on baths and single rooms.

Part III

OTHER INFORMATION

33. Crisis Procedures for Guardians

This is your immediate crisis list if you are the relative or friend of an elder and you suddenly find yourself in a guardian role. You may not have asked for this responsibility but it is yours, perhaps only for a short time.

Let's say you receive a call about an elderly relative or neighbor who is in the hospital. Your name has come up. No one knows who else to call and you are asked to help, at least until someone else can be contacted. Maybe there is no one else and you are it.

This is probably common sense but here is what has to be done:

- **Calm the elder**. Make contact with the elder if possible and assure him or her that you are there to assist with everything. Give peace of mind, and establish trust. The hospital will be examining the elder and will be surprisingly thorough. There will be a complete physical report. Perhaps the elder will be admitted for at least a short inpatient stay. This is good as it allows you time to gather loose ends.

- **Help the elder contact relatives and establish communication**. Determine who has power of attorney. Whomever is the decision maker needs to establish that at the hospital and with the rest of the relatives.

- **Help the elder apply the doctor's recommendation**. All that is needed may be a short time of supervision or assistance while the elder heals or recovers. In this case, the relatives may not arrive and take over. When the elder goes home, you will need to arrange for either an elder sitter or a series of sitters. Relatives or church members may volunteer to provide baked goods and casseroles. In this case the elder recovers independence.

However, if it is be determined that this elder can no longer live unassisted, more long-term arrangements must be made.

The rest of this list is for the legal, long-term guardian.

- **Re-determine who is in charge and what is the proposed plan**. Who will be the hands-on-support person and will there be back ups? This determination will lead to where, geographically, the elder should be lodged for the long term.

Moving an elder is almost always a setback
in mental and physical stability. Try to avoid
multiple moves.

- **Reanalyze what the elder will need**. It could
  be just group living with assistance. Because the
  elder has "fallen" and had to be rescued, it is
  more likely that twenty-four-hour care will be
  needed.

- **Resources are needed**. Locate the elder's money
  and assess its size and availability. As legal
  guardian, you need to assess the assets available
  and the ability of the elder to participate in
  decisions. Use the worksheet in chapter 11a of
  this book. Find out what income and assets there
  are, their value, and what it will take to make
  them available when needed. It may be that the
  elder's checking account will suffice for a short
  time but you need to budget for the long term. If
  for some reason, you should use your own funds
  for the elder's needs, document the expense,
  and keep receipts. Reimburse yourself as soon as
  possible, document the reimbursement, and do
  not let spending your own money become an
  expectation. If you are already on the signature
  card for the elder's account at the bank, good.
  That money is available. Use the elder's credit
  card. If you have not previously received an elder
  lawyer's counsel, get it now. Locate all power-of-
  attorney documents. Keep the family informed
  about all financial transactions and account
  balances.

- **Assess the elder's preferences.** Consider the elder's current state of awareness and the best prediction of future awareness. Do what you can to meet these needs, but when it gets to this point, you may have to give sizable consideration to conveniencing yourself, the guardian. Give the most weight to a warm, comfortable, secure place for this elder to spend his or her days.
- **Contact the elder's church.** Let the office know where the elder will be located and a mailing address, especially if the elder is active in the church and would appreciate cards or visitors.
- **Notify friends and neighbors.** Give them your name and phone number. It is amazing how an elder can disappear and no one one knows where they are or how to contact them. Be sure the elder has his or her address book, note cards, envelopes, and stamps. Locate a mail pickup and drop in the building. Help keep up correspondence as much as the elder is capable.
- **Make plans to store or distribute the elder's houshold belongings.** You don't want to maintain a residence if the elder will not return. Consider a storage facility. There may be items in a will somewhere that go to a particular person. The elder may be able to help sort out who gets what. Try to accommodate the feelings of family members; you want to keep from alienating relatives.

In the end you will have common household stuff to get rid of. Consider an estate company who will charge a percentage of the sale, say thirty percent. Second hand stores may be willing to send a truck. You will have to help box and monitor. When the elder dies, you will have to do this again with whatever is left.

34. WORKSHEET REFERENCES

AGE PREDICTION WORKSHEET

This chart is the completion of this sentence: Person 1 most clearly resembles what relative, who died of what, at the age of what. Other life-shortening factors that either you or your relative might have experienced could include: cancers, heart disease or other chronic illness that could be noted.

Also, complete the prediction for person 2.

It is only a guess, but it could be useful as you determine an approximation of how many years your estate needs to be extended.

	Person 1 (you)	Person 2 (your spouse)
Most closely resembles what relative:		
who died of:		
at age:		
Other factors:		
Cancer		
Heart		
Chronic illnesses		

Money Worksheet

Source of $$$	2 People	1st Person	2nd Person
Social Security:			
Pension #1:			
Pension #2:			
Other monthly income:			
Total monthly income:			
Investment account #1:			
Investment account #2:			
Sale of house:			
Sale of 2nd house?:			
Other assets			
Total value of assets:			

BUDGET AND RESIDENCE COMPARISON

Budget Item	Residence			
	#1	#2	#3	#4
Rent				
Utilities				
Phone				
Cable TV				
Internet				
Meals				
Garage				
Laundry				
Apartment insurance				
Auto insurance				
Prescriptions				
Health insurance				
Clothing allowance				
Entertainment				
Vacations				
Taxes on income and capital gains				

RESIDENCE EVALUATION WORKSHEET

Location, Personal Must-Haves, Residential Evaluation

This checklist is a model of the three ideas that should come together in your evaluation. Your own will have these items on it and others that are important to you.

Location:

You need to be close to _____ so the location should be _____

Alternate location:

Personal Must-Haves by priority:

1. Outside contractors allowed (if this is important to you).

2.

3.

4.

5.

6.

Evaluation of Residences:

	Res. 1	Res. 2	Res. 3
Food			
Curb appeal			
Staff attitude			
Other residents			
Money and rules			
Resident council			
Privacy and security			
Smoking			
Appropriate for you			
Intuitive choice			

PERSONAL INFORMATION WORKSHEET

Your guardian will need the following information:

Your doctor(s), name(s) and phone number(s)

Your dentist, name and phone number

Your bank, address and account number(s)

Locations of your checkbook, your driver's license, your Social Security card, and your health insurance card.

The owner name, address, and account number on your pension fund(s).

A complete list of your other accounts and investments.

Your church and the minister's name and number.

Your address book. Mark the friends you want to stay in touch with. Which ones are your best friends? Your favorite neighbors?

Location of your list of Must-Haves for residence choosing.

Location of your emergency hospital bag or box.

Location of your emergency nursing home bag or box.

35. RESOURCES

Retirement community information in your state will be available at your library and at senior centers. Also, check your telephone directory under Human Services, or Health Department, or Aging Services. Services for the aged are becoming more common. Once you have found one source, it will lead to others.

To find directories for your city, do a Web search for: directories, senior residences, your city, state.

Look for descriptions of publications that are senior directories available in print.

The following publications will aid in your search for residences or assistance in Denver, Colorado:

THE SENIORS BLUE BOOK PUBLICATION **FREE**

A North and South Metro Denver edition is published in May of each year. Libraries have them when they first come out. Later in the year you will have to contact the publisher on the web and order one. This is a 5x8 paperback, lists names, addresses, phone numbers, current prices and other amenities. This book is supported through advertising. Overall good resource.

www.SeniorsResourceGuide.com/Denver

Senior Housing Locator,

is published in the spring by
Community Housing Services, Inc. $9 in 2006
1212 Mariposa, Denver CO 80204
Call 303 831-4046 to order.

When you are doing residential comparisons this volume provides a brief, easy format. Communities are listed by geographical area by type of service. Cost ranges are included. It has some good checklists that can be photocopied.

Senior Law Handbook

A Colorado Legal Information & Reference Guide for Older Adults, published by the Colorado Bar Association. Available from Denver Regional Council Of Governments (DRCOG).

Area Agency on Aging
4500 Cherry Creek Drive South, Suite 800
Denver , CO 80246
(303) 455-1000

Retirement Living

is a handbook on choosing a retirement community published by The Jefferson County Council on Aging (JCCOA)

P.O. Box 281112
Lakewood, CO 80228
(303) 271-3487

It has detailed checklists. If you are a serious comparison shopper, this information will be helpful.

If you would like to send me your comments or suggestions, I would gladly receive them. Please include your return address.

Betty Halladay
12637 W. 6th Place
Golden Colorado 80401
jbhalladay@comcast.net